W
EVERYTHING® series!

THESE HANDY, accessible books give you all you need to tackle a difficult project, gain a new hobby, comprehend a fascinating topic, prepare for an exam, or even brush up on something you learned back in school but have since forgotten.

You can read an *EVERYTHING*® book from cover to cover or just pick out the information you want from our four useful boxes: e-facts, e-ssentials, e-alerts, and e-questions. We literally give you everything you need to know on the subject, but throw in a lot of fun stuff along the way, too.

We now have well over 150 *EVERYTHING*® books in print, spanning such wide-ranging topics as weddings, pregnancy, wine, learning guitar, one-pot cooking, managing people, and so much more. When you're done reading them all, you can finally say you know *EVERYTHING*®!

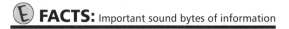
FACTS: Important sound bytes of information

ESSENTIALS: Quick and handy tips

ALERTS!: Urgent warnings

QUESTIONS: Solutions to common problems

THE EVERYTHING. Series

Dear Reader,

You are about to embark on a life-altering journey. Just by picking up this book, you've already taken the first step toward inviting more positive energy into your life.

When I first took on the adventure of writing this book, I naively thought that packing up some old belongings and moving some furniture around was all I had to do in order to apply the ancient Chinese principles of this practice called feng shui. I was wrong. Feng shui is about shifting the old mindsets that have previously blocked you. It's about making positive changes in your life in order to be in more perfect flow, harmony, and balance. It's about recognizing and respecting your place in the Universe.

Practicing feng shui decluttering will help you unearth your authentic self by removing the layers of "stuff" we tend to bury ourselves in. You can—and will—break free from the clutter that holds you back from reaching your true potential in life.

Katina Z Jones

THE
EVERYTHING®
FENG SHUI
DECLUTTERING
BOOK

Simplify your environment and your life

Katina Z. Jones

Adams Media
Avon, Massachusetts

For Simon Fu Xing, yet another blessing from China

An Everything® Series Book.
Everything® is a registered trademark of F+W Publications, Inc.

Published by Adams Media, an F+W Publications Company
57 Littlefield Street, Avon, MA 02322 U.S.A.
www.adamsmedia.com

ISBN: 1-59337-028-8
Printed in Canada.

J I H G F E D C B A

Library of Congress Cataloging-in-Publication Data
Jones, Katina Z.
The everything feng shui decluttering book / Katina Z. Jones.
p.   cm.
(An everything series book)
Includes bibliographical references.
ISBN 1-59337-028-8
1. Feng shui. I. Title. II. Series: Everything series.
BF1779.F4J663   2004
133.3'337–dc22   2003019096

This publication is designed to provide accurate and authoritative information with regard to the subject matter covered. It is sold with the understanding that the publisher is not engaged in rendering legal, accounting,
or other professional advice. If legal advice or other expert assistance is
required, the services of a competent professional person should be sought.
—From a *Declaration of Principles* jointly adopted by a Committee of the
American Bar Association and a Committee of Publishers and Associations

Many of the designations used by manufacturers and sellers to distinguish
their products are claimed as trademarks. Where those designations appear
in this book and Adams Media was aware of a trademark claim, the designations have been printed with initial capital letters.

This book is available at quantity discounts for bulk purchases.
For information, call 1-800-872-5627.

THE

EVERYTHING
Series ®

EDITORIAL

Publishing Director: Gary M. Krebs
Managing Editor: Kate McBride
Copy Chief: Laura MacLaughlin
Acquisitions Editor: Eric M. Hall
Development Editor: Larry Shea
Production Editor: Jamie Wielgus

PRODUCTION

Production Director: Susan Beale
Production Manager: Michelle Roy Kelly
Series Designer: Daria Perreault
Cover Design: Paul Beatrice and Frank Rivera
Layout and Graphics: Colleen Cunningham,
Rachael Eiben, Michelle Roy Kelly, John Paulhus
Daria Perreault, Erin Ring

Illustrations by Kathie Kelleher.
Photos by David Shoenfelt.

Visit the entire Everything® series at everything.com

Acknowledgments

Special thanks to Eric M. Hall at Adams Media; Frank Weimann of The Literary Group International; Elaine DeRosa; Kathy Baker; John Yaceczko Jr.; and my ever-growing family (especially Lilly, Madelyn, and Zoe Quan Yin) for their love, guidance, and support.

Contents

Top Ten Reasons
for Conquering Clutter

1. You will clear the space for wonderful new opportunities.

2. You'll feel less embarrassed when last-minute company arrives.

3. You'll make a better impression on business associates.

4. Your finances can improve (especially if you have a "Feng Shui Garage Sale").

5. You'll have a strong sense of peace within yourself and around your home.

6. You'll lower your stress level—improving your overall health and well-being.

7. You'll have more time for yourself—and all the things you enjoy in life.

8. You will eat more mindfully—and therefore feel healthier.

9. You'll be a model for others who are struggling with clutter issues.

10. You'll finally know where everything is!

Introduction

WHAT IS FENG SHUI, and how will it change your life? Translated literally, *feng shui* means "wind" and "water." It is a language of symbols that focus on the individual and relates everything in our space to our conscious and unconscious minds. It encompasses the forces of nature and the energies within and around us. What you learn when you practice feng shui is how to work with your intentions to attract the best things into your life, while dispersing or eliminating the negative things.

Feng shui teaches us to be sure that the things we cling to are the things we really want in our lives— because what we create in our homes symbolizes how we feel about ourselves. In actual application, feng shui practitioners use the bagua (an ancient tool) and simple psychology to help us find the positioning that works best for us—and that allows our best energy to flow freely all around us.

"Decluttering" in feng shui terms means removing the obstacles of clutter from your home—and your life. Everything we own speaks to us—and about us. How much clutter is in each room of your house? If clutter truly reflects who you are and you are okay with this, don't worry about it. But if you're like most people, you feel embarrassed or constrained by it; if it prevents you from living comfortably or makes it difficult for you to think clearly or creatively, then you should take steps to eliminate the clutter and allow the chi, or life force, to flow freely. For many people, a growing clutter problem is a direct result of an addiction to "stuff." Here are some signs that you have developed a hardcore clutter habit:

- You can't pass up the great prices at garage sales, dollar stores, and other "deals" and "steals," regardless of how much space the items consume in your home and how little you use them.
- You've run out of room in your closet, medicine cabinet, desk drawers, kitchen cabinets—just about everywhere!
- Your attic and basement are littered with boxes and bags you haven't looked at in years, including unopened boxes from the last move or two.
- Your excuse for hanging on to everything is that you never know when you might need it—even though you probably wouldn't be able to find it if some day you actually *do* need it.

Thankfully, there is a cure for addiction to "stuff," and it's simple—but it's not easy. You must say no to acquiring more useless things. Don't expect to achieve this new goal all at once. Just as with a twelve-step program, you'll have to take it one item and one day at a time. Read on, put to good use the tips on the pages that follow, and you'll be well on your way toward healthy energy or chi!

Chapter 1

Slaying the Clutter Dragon

It all starts out very innocently—a few items that you bought to decorate your home (or yourself). Nothing big, just a few "nice things" that caught your eye and that you couldn't pass up. Then a pattern begins—a few more bargains you couldn't refuse, a closet filled with clothes you might still wear when you lose those last five pounds someday, an attic full of things you haven't seen in twenty years . . .

"Just in Case"

The mighty clutter dragon has reared its ugly head and is beginning to breathe fire down your neck, usually in the form of a spouse or family member who says: "Hey, are you starting a junk store in here? Let's clean this stuff up and move some things out of here."

"No!" you cry. "I'm keeping that in case I need it later!" But when is *later*, especially when you realize that you are keeping a pair of shoes you've had since the ninth grade that you will never, ever wear again?

Simplify, Simplify

The Chinese are right when they say that a cluttered house is a cluttered mind. Chinese tradition says that the more things you own, the more problems you will have in life. Think about it: When you were in college and had basically nothing, wasn't life simpler, too? So why do you think all of the "live simpler" books have sold well in the last five years? We all seek a simpler life, yet many of us still have basements, attics, and family rooms filled with clutter.

Slaying the clutter dragon is actually an easy thing to do—all it takes is a new perspective, a new way of taking a hard look at yourself and honestly assessing what you truly need in life.

The American Way

A woman who has recently been to China gave the best travel advice for almost any trip: "Don't pack more than you can comfortably hold in a carry-on bag.

Americans are notorious for packing more in one large suitcase than an entire Chinese family typically owns!" She was not aware of the feng shui significance her advice implied. But the truth is, most Chinese families (except for the fabulously wealthy) have a very limited need for things. They tend to have only the most necessary, basic items on hand: a bed, a couch, a kitchen table, some dishes, and silverware. Seldom will you see more than one of anything in their homes.

 ESSENTIAL

Keeping things that are broken, useless, or obsolete is not practicing good feng shui. In good feng shui, everything you own should provide some kind of service to you—otherwise you will become a slave to it.

The need for many things is a well-established American trait—and it can easily go from just a bad habit to a fixation that is difficult to get over. Look at the success of eBay, which lists more than a million items for sale by their owners on a daily basis. That's a lot of stuff!

It seems unavoidable—every day, people are inundated with more and more opportunities to buy things that will supposedly enhance their lives. The overwhelming accumulation of stuff just seems to happen, but the reality is that you have much more control over your excesses than you think. Western culture has placed such an emphasis on materialism that people actually believe they need more than they do.

Every day, it becomes harder and harder to simplify, to accept life as it is right now, at this moment . . . and to back down from the infinite opportunities to "improve" it. Practice saying no to things for one day, and you'll see what conscious effort it requires.

When Your Cup Runneth Over

Most people believe that he who dies with the most toys wins. Watching TV commercials for a day will show you just how strongly people are pushed to become obsessed with possessions. In a decidedly unscientific experiment, a few hours of television included seventeen commercials that said viewers were absolutely nothing without the right hair color, the right car, the right home, and all the best new toys and foods. People are hit with similar images repeatedly throughout the day in everything from radio shows to billboards and shopping cart ads.

How can you tell if you've attained official pack-rat status? Look for the telltale signs:

- Bookshelves are overstuffed receptacles for many things, only half of which are actually books.
- Clothes overflow from your closet and land in piles on the floor, chair, treadmill, or dressing table.
- Kitchen "junk" drawers are filled so high they do not shut properly.

- Pantries are full of food you no longer like to eat.
- Medicine chests are filled with old or expired medications.
- Desks are crammed with papers so old you are no longer sure of their need or meaning.
- You have a collection of broken items you are keeping to fix later, when you have time.
- You keep anything long past its shelf life or usefulness.

It might be a good idea to do a clutter check before embarking on a fresh new journey through feng shui. The previous list identifies common trouble spots. Find the clutter traps in your own environment, make a list of them, and use it at the start of each new season. Take a good look around, regularly, to be sure you're not creating blockages in your life by adding clutter in areas where you definitely don't want or need it.

What Clutter Really Means

You probably don't realize that much of this clutter is a sign of a real emotional, though no longer useful, attachment. When you begin to clear the clutter in your home, you also begin to release old attachments to things that no longer serve you or bring you joy.

For instance, you might be keeping an old pair of tennis shoes that you wore on a favorite date, but since the relationship ultimately didn't work out, keeping the shoes is hanging on to something that is no longer part of your life. Such tendencies can hold you back from a rewarding new relationship, because—psychologically speaking—you are holding on to the past.

When you begin to clear away years' worth of clutter from your attic, you may be amazed by how much stuff from your past has been holding you back from your future. Since the attic represents higher goals or aspirations, it's no wonder you may feel like you haven't achieved all you were capable of in life. That's what good feng shui does—it makes you start making conscious decisions based on your true intentions.

Fear and Hoarding

Don't underestimate the power of fear. As you walk through piles of old clothes, record albums, books, and knickknacks, you may ask yourself why you've been keeping all of these things for so long. Did you expect to use them again one day? Not likely. Instead, you probably hadn't felt ready to relinquish your past due to your uncertainty regarding your future.

Between changing jobs, repeated moves, or various stages of marriage, the possibility of not having enough to survive is a very real concern for many people. Individuals in a state of continual change often take comfort in emotional hoarding. They collect things to pacify a soul that is yearning for love, hoping for the kind of satisfaction that money can't buy. Often, they don't realize what they are doing until they have so much stuff in their homes that they can hardly breathe! For good feng shui in your home, you must take a good hard look at yourself and your needs—and purge the items that no longer serve you.

 ESSENTIAL

> The best litmus test for elimination of clutter is to look at each item and ask yourself, "When was the last time I used this?" If it was more than a year ago, it's probably not an essential item in your life. It might be of better use to someone else.

When you really listen to others talk about their clutter (not that they would call it "clutter"), you may notice that their attachment to it almost always has its roots in a fear of not having enough to survive. Although many of these people were born after the Great Depression in the 1930s, their parents carried (and passed on) a "poverty consciousness" based upon their own experience and worries during their own family's struggle for survival.

Emotional hoarding is not limited to possessions; the same principles of feng shui clearing apply to the "clutter" people pack into their bodies. It's no accident that overweight people suffer from the same emotional issues as other types of hoarders and are affected by the same worry of not having enough. What's really interesting is that when hoarders and clutter-a-holics begin to practice good feng shui and relinquish their piles of clutter, many also begin to lose weight!

A Constant Process

Incorporating feng shui into your lifestyle and mind-set is an ongoing process. It may be years before you realize that you are happy, secure, and certain. Continually evaluate where you are and what you need, and soon you will be facing down the clutter dragon. You will know that it is definitely time for a major purging, both physically and psychologically—and what a fabulous feeling it will be to finally liberate yourself from your fears or failures of the past!

As you take a deeper look into the psychological ties you've had to the past, don't forget to check out the other clutter traps in your home. Think about clutter in the garage, basement, hall closet, and even in your car. Looking more deeply at the situation, what can you learn about your clutter patterns? Lots of things—for instance, the clutter in your basement—symbolizes some uneasiness in your family situation, since the basement in feng shui is symbolic of family and strong foundations.

Clutter in the garage can signify a psychological difficulty in leaving your house every day—or in coming home. If you block yourself out of your garage with clutter, you might ask yourself what it is you are having difficulty returning to in your home life. Conversely, if you are a real homebody and barricade yourself into your garage with clutter, maybe it's time to consider starting a home-based business so you can spend more time at home but in a healthier manner.

The key to dealing with clutter is to be able to take these kinds of hard looks at yourself, your needs, and your motivations in order to find out why you are keeping what you are keeping. Once you understand your motivations, you can eliminate the clutter for good—and greatly improve your inner sense of well-being in the meantime.

 QUESTION

What is emotional hoarding?
Emotional hoarding is the collecting of things to satisfy the soul's need for comfort, security, love, or other intangibles that money can't buy.

Prosperity and Abundance

A central aspect to the study of feng shui, and metaphysics in general, is the concept of *continual abundance*. Through *prosperity consciousness*, as it is also called, the more you give the more you are open to receive. There is no such thing as, "I may need it someday," because as soon as you give something away, you create a space for whatever is new and needed at the moment. If you give in to the worry about never having enough, you will create a life in which you really can never have enough to be happy.

Instead, reframe your thinking to accept yourself where you are now in your life. You will always be prosperous because you will attract positive abundance. It's such a simple concept, yet difficult for most to master without consistent (and committed) practice. It may take several years to look at yourself, and your life, from this perspective on a regular basis.

One of the basic laws of metaphysics (often thought of as the workings of karma) is that what you put out to the Universe is what you will receive back. So, if you tell the Universe that you expect to be poor and unhealthy, that is the life you will create for yourself just from your own limiting state of mind. The real magic of life comes from your own beliefs about what you think you can achieve.

Dealing with a Clutter-a-holic

The piles sit on the floor, are tucked (or stuffed) under furniture, or are balanced precariously in a corner. You want to clean them up, but there's a problem: None of this stuff is yours; it's somebody else's pile of clutter.

What can you do? Begin by approaching the person in a friendly manner and offering to help him or her put the items away. People are fiercely protective of their things, so don't just start putting things away, or (worse yet) start pitching them in the trash. Respect your partner's or family member's need for some privacy—and ownership.

Try to get to the root of the problem by asking some simple questions: "Does this still serve a purpose for you? Does it bring you joy or have special meaning? If so, we can find a special place for it. If not, maybe we can donate it so that someone else can use it."

Take the lead by becoming a positive, shining example. When you clear your own clutter, you may inspire those around you to be tidy, too. If your kitchen table is stacked high with mail or projects, on the other hand, it won't even be noticeable if someone adds a lunch box or an extra set of keys to your pile of clutter.

One practical suggestion: Create opportunities for storage solutions by placing a "collection container" in hallways or closets. If there is a designated place for clutter collection, the clutter will become part of a more organized thought process—the first step toward elimination!

 ALERT

When cleaning your house, don't forget dirt and dust traps such as windowsills, molding, chair rails, and light fixtures. Dust and dirt hold chi down.

Staying positive and focusing on solutions will go a long way toward quickly clearing clutter, yours and others. Don't interfere too much with other people's purging process, especially if they seem reluctant at first. Inspire them by setting a good and lasting example of a person who is free from the binding nature of "too many things." It's just like Gandhi said: "You must be the change you want to see."

Other Kinds of Clutter

Okay, let's say you've cleared the clutter in your attic, garage, and basement and the rest of your home is sparkling clean. Now you're all ready for some feng shui, right?

Not necessarily. There are other kinds of clutter besides physical clutter, and though they might not be as obvious, they can create obstacles in your life nonetheless.

- **Time clutter** occurs when you fill up your schedule with too many commitments, and then have too little time left over for your family or social life. You should always leave "open" time to allow for new opportunities to learn and grow.
- **Mind clutter** happens when you allow your brain to fill with thoughts, worries, and concerns about the future. To alleviate this kind of clutter, consider keeping a journal. Writing down your thoughts is a positive, healthy way to get worries and other forms of mental clutter out of your mind and into a safe, directed place.
- **Electronic clutter** is another insidious form of clutter that can block chi. Right at this moment, you may be saving dozens of useless old e-mails or voice mail messages; maybe you have a computer hard drive you haven't cleaned up since 1997. You should clear as much as you can in your "virtual" world on a daily basis.

- **Food clutter** consists of consuming more than your body needs, or keeping more food than you or your family will ever eat. One sign that you have this problem is if you constantly have to throw away uneaten food that has spoiled.

Clearing your mind—whether it's cluttered by worry, food, or overbooking—is necessary for your personal chi, and a very healthy thing to do. If journaling seems like it might take too much time, try a "Thoughts and Worries" jar with little slips of paper containing your concerns. What you're doing, of course, is giving your anxiety clutter another place to live. Here's another way to purge those concerns that aren't helping you: Get into a quiet space, breathe deeply, and mentally hit the "delete" key in your brain to rid yourself of negativity!

Clearing the Air

The most important thing about clearing clutter of all kinds is to recognize that it is necessary in order to wipe your energy slate clean, so to speak. You want to start rearranging your home and surroundings in the most positive, unaffected way possible—and clutter blocks any and all good energy from flowing positively through your personal environment. It is the root of all "chi" problems, and while using this book will help you overcome binding clutter for good, it might be helpful on your life-altering journey to learn more about the basics of good feng shui.

Chapter 2

The Basics: Goals of Feng Shui

*F*eng shui literally means "wind and water." Wind moves the invisible life force called *chi*, and water retains or cultivates it. An ancient Chinese system, feng shui teaches people how to create harmony between nature and manmade structures. Traditional practitioners of feng shui believe that this "intentional harmony" will balance out the world, bringing peace and prosperity to all. Many people today are exploring feng shui as a way to bring balance to their own life and spirit.

The Mother of Invention

Thousands of years ago, in southern China (a rich, fertile region of mountains, rivers, valleys, and farms), the art of feng shui was born out of necessity. People had a real need to determine the most auspicious places for their homes, altars, and burial grounds. The burial sites were particularly important to the people, since they relied heavily upon the energy of their ancestors for everything from good crops and increased prosperity to spiritual guidance.

To these primitive yet wise rural people, everything spiritual and ethereal had its own earthly correspondent in nature, and everything in nature could be carefully "directed" to assist in the achievement of earthly goals. What were (and are) those goals? Simply put, to achieve a positive flow of energy, a balance of the eternal opposites of yin and yang, and a proper interaction of the five elements (fire, earth, metal, water, and wood).

 QUESTION

What is feng shui?
Feng shui means, literally, "wind and water." The practice of feng shui relates to the positive flow of energy through your indoor, outdoor, and spiritual surroundings. Contrary to popular belief, it isn't just about moving furniture around to attract wealth!

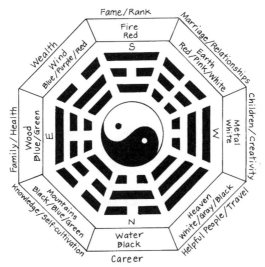

The Bagua: To use the bagua, place the career side along the entrance of your space (which can be as general as your yard or as focused as your desk). That is your starting point.

Although we are many miles and several centuries away from the original feng shui "masters," we share a common belief today that external factors affect our internal landscapes, whether for good or ill.

We know that there are invisible cosmic forces that govern all things—man, nature, and the Universe—and the main goal of feng shui is to learn to move gracefully within this flow. It's definitely not a religion, and it's not about moving some stuff out of your house so you can go get more stuff. In feng shui, it's the energy or chi that counts most, followed by good intentions and personal integrity. It also requires an open mind, one that can take an objective and honest look around at its surroundings and be ready to give up in order to receive.

Do you need to practice the principles of good feng shui in every single room of your house? No, you don't. But remember—the more that you create using feng shui principles in your life, the better your overall results are likely to be.

The Feng Shui "Schools"

Today, there are many individual schools of feng shui, and many different methods that practitioners use to help others move their possessions and elements in the right direction. However, most feng shui practice can be divided into the following three basic schools.

Form School

The Form School began in rural southern China and focuses on the lay of the land (i.e., landforms), water formations, and the topography of the land. Practitioners of this school will generally spend most of their time evaluating the lot your home is situated on and the relationship of each area of your home to the land surrounding it.

Compass School

In northern China, where there weren't as many hills, people devised a more scientific method of finding the right directions for homes, people, and possessions: They created a compass called the "luo pan." Many places of the world use this method, but because it requires use of a compass and some mathematical prowess, many Westerners find it too complicated to use. If this school is appealing to you, your best bet is to find a practitioner who is skilled in the Compass School—attempting to use the compass on your own could result in inaccurate readings or results.

Black Hat (or Buddhist) Sect

Founded by Professor Thomas Lin Yun, the Black Hat Sect (or School) synthesizes Buddhism, Taoism, shamanism, and folk wisdom. It encourages anyone who practices feng shui, professional or novice, to rely heavily upon intuition. The only feng shui tool a Black Hat practitioner uses is the bagua. In the Black Hat Sect, if it feels right, it probably is—as long as there is a positive, healthy flow of chi. Black Hat also incorporates the Zen practice of meditation.

This book will focus mostly on the Black Hat Sect of feng shui, as it is the easiest of the three schools for the novice to effectively follow and implement in his surroundings.

The Balance of Yin and Yang

The concept of yin and yang, the eternal opposites, is common to all schools of feng shui study and practice. Chances are, you've even heard the saying, "It's a yin-yang thing." But what exactly are yin and yang—and how do they work in the world of feng shui? In their simplest sense, they represent two opposing yet complementary halves of a whole—the duality of the Universe.

"Yin" is the female energy, which is soft, nurturing, flowing, passive, and contemplative. Its direction is north, the numbers associated with it are even, and its universal correspondent is earth. "Yang" is the male, or aggressive, energy and is bright, solid, and creative. Yang represents odd numbers, the southern direction, and the energy of heaven. Together, the two symbols form a whole circle and the complete Universe—but each has a dot in it of the other's energy, meaning there is some yin in yang and some yang in yin to complete the whole picture.

 FACT

Yin is earth energy (feminine, passive energy), and yang is heaven energy (masculine, dynamic energy). The yin-yang symbol is round, continuous, and complementary—both energies are needed in balanced form to create wholeness. Neither is better than the other.

The symbol of yin and yang shows us that we should seek the natural balance in all things, and that all things, both natural and manmade, naturally gravitate toward this balance. The same is true in human beings, all of whom contain a little of the opposite sex's energy in them. How many times have you heard someone say, "Wow, that man is really in touch with his feminine side?" or "She has a male strength about her." What people are really responding to when they say things like that is the complementary nature of energies in another that set them apart or help them to achieve admirable feats—well-balanced people are admirable!

With yin and yang, the object is to keep the balance as, well, balanced, as possible—to not have rooms or living spaces that are too yin or too yang. The mission of feng shui is to seek out that balance in each room so you can help yourself feel grounded or centered in your living environment.

The Five Elements

A key to understanding feng shui is learning about the five elements (fire, earth, metal, water, and wood) and discovering how they relate to one another in ways that mimic nature. As in nature, there are both creative and destructive cycles, and here's the "magic formula" for each:

- **Creative cycle:** Fire creates earth, earth creates metal, metal creates water, water creates wood, and wood creates fire.
- **Destructive cycle:** Fire melts metal, metal cuts wood, wood moves earth, earth muddies water, and water puts out fire.

The Chinese believe that the Universe is heavily influenced by this positive and negative (yin-yang) interaction of the five elements. A room that uses good feng shui placement has a balanced use of each element— and is not too heavy on any one element. Too much of one element (especially a powerful one like fire) can make a room feel oppressive and can actually block the chi of the home's inhabitants.

ESSENTIAL

Good feng shui takes some time to get used to—and to take effect. Give your efforts some "breathing time" before you start expecting miracles. The best feng shui practitioners will tell you that some results will feel instant, while others will take time and may require some refining to achieve.

Elemental Qualities

On a symbolic level, the elements represent order and the influence of the Universe in nature and all things, including humankind.

But let's look more closely at the qualities associated with each element for an even deeper understanding:

Fire represents emotions and corresponds to the color red. Fire energy is pure yang—strong, assertive, and dominant. In objects for décor, real fire elements such as candles or oil lamps can be used to represent the fire element in a room. Or you can use symbolic items like a red star, red fabric, or even red flowers.

Earth relates very much to the physical plane of existence. In people, earth types are grounded, organized, and very practical in all matters. They are quite levelheaded and hold harmony very dear to their hearts. Earth elements that can be used in décor include soil in a potted plant, yellow and brown items, or rectangular objects like a flowerbed that fits on a windowsill.

Metal energy pertains to mental activity and thought processes. Use metal objects like metal picture frames, lampposts, sculptures, or clocks in a room to represent this pensive energy. Symbolically, you can use round items that are silver, gold, or white in color to represent metal. Just remember that the closer the object is to its natural element, the stronger the energy of the object in your home will be. The more symbolic you get, the less powerful the object will be in positively affecting your home situation.

 ALERT

Begin your feng shui process with a clear idea of your intention. Everything about your process should be geared toward the positive, from your initial attitude to the finishing touches. Never begin on a negative note (i.e., with a plan to use feng shui to ward off evil neighbors).

Water relates to spirituality, reflection, and meditation. There is always an air of mystery with water elements. To incorporate water into your home, use clear glass vases or pitchers with fresh water, glass or clear marble stones in a dish or bowl, or anything black (since black is the symbolic color of water). You can also use a fountain or aquarium to add the water element to a room.

Wood relates to intuition and the feeling of "knowingness" inside us all. Wood people are strong yet flexible, trusting their inner voice to lead them to the next project or situation safely. Best to use real live plants in your home décor to represent wood; bamboo sticks are especially considered in feng shui to be auspicious, or full of good luck. Anything green will symbolically create the wood element in your home.

Each of the above elements is represented on the bagua (see "Feng Shui's Energy Map" later in this chapter). The most important thing to remember about the elements is that you need to keep them balanced. Don't worry if you don't understand it all yet. When we go room by room later in the book, there will be plenty of good examples to make everything clear!

Sensory Connection

Also key to the principles of good feng shui is the need to balance appeal to all of the senses. After all, the senses are considered to be the human manifestation of the five elements. But how can you accomplish a balance of these energies in your home? Here's an example of how it can work. You will have a well-balanced living room if you include items that appeal to each of your senses: a scented candle (smell), soft pillows on the sofa (touch), fresh fruit in a bowl (taste), soft music or a gently splashing water fountain (sound), and an interesting, dynamic piece of artwork hanging on one of the walls (sight).

Every room of the house can use this kind of attention to its balance of the senses. Don't be afraid to think a little unconventionally—you can incorporate taste into your bathroom "spa" experience by mixing up a fresh fruit smoothie to sip on during your bath.

Feng Shui's Energy Map

If feng shui is a way of life, then the bagua (see diagram on page 17) is the road map for getting to all the great places you want to be in life. Each of your endeavors is represented in a corner of the octagon, and each corner also has its corresponding colors, elements, and energy.

Used correctly, the bagua helps you to determine the preferred locations for all of your beloved possessions. Ancient Chinese wisdom holds the belief that when we place items carefully and with intention, we clear away the blockages of energy that can hold us back from success. In other words, it's how you keep your stuff that determines how well you do in life.

Simply translated, *bagua* means eight-sided figure or octagon. It comes from a book of ancient Chinese wisdom called the I Ching, or the "Book of Changes." The "Book of Changes" is a method of divination that contains insightful and profound teachings in the form of trigrams, which are symbols pertaining to business, life, and the ways of nature and the Universe. The I Ching reveals the flow of nature as perfect balance (yin-yang) and harmony.

Each area of the bagua has a connection with the main aspects of your life: career, helpful people (who assist in creating opportunities and good luck), children/creativity, relationship/marriage, fame/reputation, wealth/abundance, family/health/well-being, and knowledge/self-cultivation. In feng shui, all of these "channels" are affected by both positive and negative (or blocked) energies; the goal is to keep the energies as positive and flowing as possible.

 ESSENTIAL

Go easy on yourself and your surroundings at first. Assess your current living situation with a positive checklist rather than a guilt-ridden list of what's wrong. Remember to stay positive throughout the process—this includes being positive toward yourself!

As a tool, the bagua is placed over your location so each area of your home or business has meaning. For example, one area represents wealth, and another, partnership. As these sections of your location represent areas of your life, you have the potential to transform your life situation when you activate them in alignment with your clearly stated intention.

The Sections of the Bagua

To use the bagua, you need to place it (either physically or using your visualization ability) over the main entrance to your home with the career side aligned with the front wall. The area of career is always at the front of the location; this means that your front door is usually in the section of knowledge, career, or helpful people.

- **Career** represents how you serve community and family. This part of the bagua demonstrates your expression in the world of work, whether as an employee, entrepreneur, or volunteer.
- **Helpful people** represents teachers, mentors, helpers in life, friends, angels (as spiritual "helpers"), and opportunities brought through chance meetings. It is sometimes called the "Gate of Heaven" and is the method by which luck comes into your life.
- **Children and creativity** represents all children and the incubation-like process of creativity. The creative process is key to your personal, spiritual, and psychological growth, and is absolutely critical to your career success if you are a writer, artist, or creative type.

- **Relationship** represents the important relationships (including marriage) of the inhabitants of the house. For a business, it represents the partners involved in running the business. The relationship corner is where you'll want to support a present relationship or conjure a new one by placing things in pairs.

- **Fame** represents reputation, image, and how others see us in the world. Our ability to generate fame and success in business and in life depends heavily on the integrity of our intentions.

- **Wealth** represents the "ka-ching" factor in our lives, or our ability to earn, keep, and grow money. But it can also represent abundance in all things, not just the material.

- **Family** represents a loving, supporting family well rooted in ancestry. It also supports your interaction with your community of friends with whom you gather and may have like interests. If the location is an office, it supports a community atmosphere and people working in harmony.

   Health represents the individual and collective health of all living beings—including pets and plants—in a building such as your home.

- **Knowledge** represents wisdom and the ability to acquire new knowledge. The knowledge area also supports a total path of self-knowledge and spiritual awareness. In this area of the bagua, self-help books are quite welcome.

Place the bagua over geographic areas in your house (either over your whole floor plan or just room by room), then look at its corresponding life endeavor. As a map, of sorts, the bagua will help you determine the most auspicious locations and décor to help you achieve your life's goals. Remember, you don't have to apply feng shui to every single room, but the more attention and mindfulness you give to each part of your surroundings, the better the results will be.

 ESSENTIAL

Balance the yin energies (feminine, curving, nurturing, dark, soft, earthly energy) with the yang (masculine, active, angular, sharp, heaven, and sun energy) to achieve a balance that will make you feel most comfortable in a space.

Does Your Home Reflect Your Life?

What does your home say about you? If you try to view your home through the eyes of a stranger—considering the arrangement of each room, the amount of clutter or the lack thereof, the colors, the textures, the scents and sights—what do you think your home reveals?

Evaluating Clutter

How much clutter is in each room of your house? Is the clutter reflective of your personality? A teenager may defend the piles of clothes, books, papers, and other odds and ends in his room as providing comfort and security for him. "It's who I am," he will say defiantly when asked why he seems to enjoy this environment. If clutter truly reflects who you are, don't worry about it. But if you feel embarrassed by it, or, worse, constrained by it, pay attention to this cue; if it prevents your living comfortably, keeps you awake at night, or prevents you from thinking clearly or creatively, then you should take steps to eliminate the clutter and allow the chi to flow freely.

 ALERT

Work on one room or area of your house at a time. Do not try to feng shui your whole house in one weekend. It takes plenty of "reflective time" to consider your actions and to determine the changes that will feel best.

A Feeling of Welcome

Conversely, are your rooms too spare? Are the walls white and bare, the furniture sterile, and the space too pristine? Are guests afraid to sit or move about freely in the room or rooms for fear of making a mess or disturbing the arrangement in some way? Do you cover your furniture with plastic or rush to place coasters under every cup and glass? In other words, are you projecting unfriendliness and a "keep out" mentality to others? This is fine if you truly do not want guests showing up on your doorstep. However, if you are having trouble attracting friends to your home or keeping them there long once they arrive, it could be because the starkness of your decor or the sparseness of your furnishings is pushing them away.

Room for Children

Is your home completely open to your children, or have you relegated their toys, books, and other possessions to only a room or two? Is there anything at all that is welcoming or comforting to children in the living room, the dining room, the patio, or the den?

Allowing them even a little space throughout the house and a place for them to play in most, if not all, of the rooms gives children the comfort of knowing that the home is theirs, too. Providing child-sized furniture and allowing a few toys in even the neatest and most sophisticated of rooms tells others that there is room in your life and your heart for something much more important than material possessions—your children.

Allowing the Energy to Flow

Is your home open, airy, and filled with light, or packed with possessions, close, and dark? Are the colors rich and vibrant in the rooms where you spend your waking hours and soft and relaxing in the rooms where you sleep or unwind? Can chi move easily through your rooms and hallways? Do you demonstrate awareness of the bagua in how your furnishings are arranged? Can the flow of energy in your home be improved by making minor adjustments in one or more rooms, or even in the yard or garden?

Once you become aware of these principles of feng shui, you will see that it is not difficult to change aspects of your home and property in order to improve energy flow and open up your life to the positive results that will follow! Of course, your starting point will be the removal of clutter—the great energy block—from your life.

Good Vibrations Energy Audit

Before you embark on your feng shui journey, it's a good idea to conduct an "energy audit" to determine areas of clear and blocked chi. Here's a quick checklist for assessing the chi in and around your home:

1. Is the path to your front door open, curved, and inviting? In good feng shui, your doorway should be clear and unencumbered.
2. Does your front door open to a staircase that goes up or down? Chi comes in through your front door and should be able to move through your house slowly. If your staircase is in direct line with the front door, the chi rushes up the stairs and back out of the house—especially if there is a small window at the top of the staircase. Hang a crystal to slow down the chi.
3. In your living room, does the air feel stagnant? That's a sign that the energy in the room is blocked. Open some windows or use a ceiling fan

to circulate the chi in the room—and bring some life back to the living room.

4. Do the hallways seem open and airy? Are there piles of clutter stacked in a hallway "loading dock" (i.e., waiting for a move to storage that never seems to happen)?

Start with a Clean Space

Before you begin the process of changing your home's energy, be sure to begin with a space clearing. If weather permits, open windows to get the chi moving. Physically clean the space you will be working on. Dirt and dust symbolize stagnant chi—and that must always be cleared first!

Clearing the Way

Light a candle (a pure aromatherapy type), diffuse pure essential oils, burn incense, or use a smudge stick (a tightly wrapped bundle of herbs and wood). Just be sure that whatever you use is in its purest form. Unfortunately, there are a lot of products on the market today that claim to be pure aromatherapy that are, in fact, full of artificial fillers and additives.

Play some music. A wonderful drumming or chanting CD would be great, but use what you love the most. It doesn't have to be meditation music to "speak" to you—and there's nothing like a little Tina Turner or Rolling Stones to get the chi moving!

ESSENTIAL

> Always begin with a close look at your intentions. What do you want to accomplish? What are your goals, and which are most important to you right now? What action are you preparing yourself to take?

The Right Intentions

Now you're ready for step two, which is *intention*. Remember your intention as you're placing the appropriate enhancement or cure in a particular sector. Keep this intention clearly in your mind. Open your heart to your highest good. Embrace the possibilities, and most important, trust your process.

The final step involves reinforcing all that you have done—giving more power to your enhancement or cure. This is the part where you meditate and offer blessings or thanks to the Universe through a process the Black Hat Sect of feng shui calls "The Three Secrets":

1. *Mudra* (hand gesture) is often the position of prayer, with both palms together, fingers pointing up. Hold your hands to your heart.
2. *Mantra* (prayer) is the prayer or blessing you are most comfortable with. It could be as simple as "Thy will be done," or maybe a simple prayer you've written on your own. Whatever the case,

recite it nine times. Nine is an auspicious number in feng shui.

3. *Visualization of your specific intention:* As you recite your mantra and hold your hands in the mudra position, hold your intention in your mind's eye the entire time, as though it has already been accomplished. Use affirmative statements with this visualization (i.e., "I have already created space for love in my life" or "I am surrounded by a loving family").

Chances are, you'll feel uplifted and ready to take on the world when you're finished with these steps. But don't forget the last step of the whole process: Let go of the outcome—and trust the Universe to do its work!

The Eight Remedies or Cures

Adding remedies to a specific area where the chi seems to be blocked is the best way to open up the energy to its greatest good. In feng shui, there are eight basic remedies or cures:

- **Light**—includes lighting, mirrors, candles, and reflective surfaces.
- **Sound**—wind chimes, bells, and hollow bamboo flutes. Anything that sounds harmonious (such as music or chanting) can also work as a cure.
- **Color**—Red and black in particular can be used to stimulate the flow of chi.
- **Life**—Living objects, such as pets or plants, can also get the chi moving in your home or surroundings.

- **Movement**—Flags, ribbons, banners, fountains, wind chimes, weather vanes, or hanging crystals are cures associated with movement.
- **Stillness**—When chi moves too quickly, you need to slow it down with still objects such as statues or large rocks.
- **Mechanical/electrical**—This can mean machinery, but be careful that your electrical items don't over-stimulate the chi. Too much energy defeats the purpose of a cure.
- **Straight lines**—It's best here to use scrolls, swords, flutes, bamboo sticks, and fans.

Using Total Feng Shui

Harness the subtle power of feng shui and its cures to move yourself in the right spiritual direction. Your feng shui mantra should be: "Trust the Universe." In short, trust your intuition. Let go of the outcome. Give thanks for all that is.

Learn to "mindfully move" the items in your environment that are creating obstacles in your life. Obstacles are not only physical items such as a couch, table, or computer, but also the mental "clutter" that keeps you from practicing mindfulness and holds you back from achieving your greatest potential in life.

Now, roll up your silk sleeves, put on some soft Chinese bamboo flute music, and get started!

Chapter 3
Free-Chi Paths

Beginning at the end of your driveway, the life force known as chi follows a path that leads it to your front door, into your home, through the hallway arteries to all of your rooms, and then out the back door. Ideally, chi shouldn't encounter obstacles along the way. Clutter is one of the main sources of blockages that can upset the course of free-flowing chi and cause your home to be stagnant and out of balance.

Going with the Flow

The primary life force that surrounds us all is the sun. But the wind is what moves the invisible energy force, or chi, around us in a way that the ancient Chinese believed would breathe health and happiness into our lives. Remember, "feng shui" means "wind and water," both nature elements that "flow" energy into our environments. Like ripples of water flowing toward us, positive chi energy can wash over us, revitalizing our spirits, but can also dissipate quickly, especially when it hits an obstacle. The key is to keep paths open to allow the chi to replenish itself along its unencumbered path.

Chi can encounter many outside forces along the path to your front door: land formations such as hills or large rocks, plants and vegetation, small bodies of water, or the clutter from your everyday life. What kinds of clutter might be in the way of chi? How about kids' toys, gardening tools, patio furniture, yard decorations, and even that rusty old car you can no longer drive? All of these items can block the positive chi from entering (and blessing) your home.

Even today, many Chinese believe that all possessions, whether inside or outside of the home, are symbolic of our chances and opportunities in life and that too much junk along the path to your home can literally choke your potential. But think about the logic behind the symbolism: Clearing your driveway will enable you to freely come and go from your home, creating a free and easy path to and from work each day. Not having to worry about whether you're backing over

Junior's tricycle or that new tray of flowers you just purchased but haven't had time to plant can be a wonderful way to start (and end) each day! Store the driveway clutter on shelves in the garage where possible, and pitch the old stuff you're no longer using.

 ESSENTIAL

> Clutter can mimic the path of chi into and through your home. Like a tornado, it can follow the chi in through you and your family members—leaving its own "path of destruction" near doorways, in hallways, and on staircases. These are all prime areas where chi must be allowed to flow most freely.

The Front Door: Where All Paths Lead

The path to your front door represents your health and well-being to the rest of the world. Even too much of good things like plants and interesting yard decorations can point to a deeper lack of self-confidence—or a fear of not having enough. Do you care too much about material things, or about how others perceive you? Be careful what you show to outsiders on their path to your front door.

An Open-Door Policy

Once you open the door, note whether it opens nice and wide. It should, so that your opportunities have the most room to enter your home. If your door is too tight, you might discover that your opportunities are also limited. If you have a screen door, keep your main door behind it wide open as often as you can; this will let in the maximum amount of light, and it will signify to the world that you're ready for new and wonderful things to happen!

But before swinging your door wide open to welcome guests, be sure there's no clutter behind it. Because of its location as the primary entrance to your home, it is likely the primary dumping ground for coats, shoes, bookbags, packages, mail, and much more than you can even imagine. Is this the first impression you most want to leave on your guests? Probably not—so deal with this clutter by adding coatracks, shelving in your hall closet, and a basket to help you organize your incoming mail. For school projects and related papers, create an "in" basket by attaching plastic file shelving to the inside of the closet door. Here, papers can be stored in an orderly, "out-of-sight" manner until a time when you can later sort through them.

If your door opens to a straight path leading back out of the house via a back door, you have the feng shui challenge of "rushing chi" to contend with, so here it would be okay to create a few intentional boundaries along that path to slow down the energy and allow your opportunities to linger a spell. You can place a small water fountain near the front door, or perhaps a pillar with a plant on it in the hallway. If it is big enough to divert your eye's attention, it's big enough to slow down the chi. You can also use a screen or a wind chime to slow down the energy.

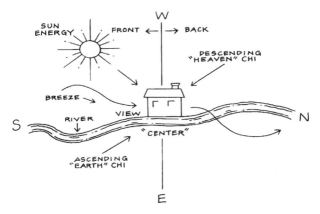

Yard Full of Chi: The ideal home location will maximize the flow of every kind of energy. This house is located in the center of the property, facing south. The hill to the north brings dragon energy down from heaven (and guards the rear). The slope up to the front of the house carries chi from the earth.

Step Inside This House

Much like the front door projects an image of you to the rest of the world, your entranceway or foyer reflects the image of who you are *into* your house. It picks up on the energy of the front door and brings that image right on inside.

The entrance is still part of the mouth of chi, so it's important to keep the airways open in the entranceway so that good chi can "breathe" throughout your home. If you have a large entrance to your home, you won't have to do much to enhance this area from a feng shui standpoint. But if your entrance is narrow, you would greatly benefit from a metal wind chime hung from the ceiling. The door, when opened, will immediately start circulating the chi, sending it out from your entrance to all areas of your home.

 QUESTION

What is chi?
Chi is the Americanized phonetic spelling of *qi,* the force of life that flows through objects and nature in general. Chi flows through your life, and your surroundings. The goal of feng shui is to direct chi in a more positively flowing manner.

If there's a window near your entrance, make sure you slow down the chi with some billowy curtains, mini-blinds, or a plant in front of the window, especially if you've got a wind chime helping to spread good chi. You don't want it to go running out the window, do you?

What's Behind Door #2?

Let's face it: Most closets are scary places. Sure, they can be neat and orderly storage places for our most useful possessions (like raincoats, boots, hats, gloves, and winter apparel), but more likely they are the museum of many things we no longer use—or worse yet, have no idea what to do with anymore. Just how many coats does a person really need to have in his closet?

Since they are convenient hideaways for everything that would normally clutter our hallways, closets can become the storage hot spot for things that really belong in other rooms of our homes—or, better yet, in the trash bin. We are always one unexpected guest away from stashing more stuff than belongs in there, and typically one full weekend away from clearing it out again afterward.

But why should the closet be any different from any other room of your home? It's just a smaller version of other rooms, only it is a space that's specifically designated to store things that would be clutter elsewhere. However, this doesn't mean you should pile papers, knickknacks, old shoes, gardening tools, and more from the floor to the coatrack inside your closet. Rather, you should carefully place items that you need for the current season so that they are readily accessible, and be sure to leave enough room for your guests to hang their coats as well. Off-season coats and accessories should be stored in plastic containers in your attic or basement until the seasons change and they become appropriate again.

One of the main reasons closets become stuffed well beyond their capacity to close is that people have a tendency to hang onto old coats that are no longer worn but carry some kind of memory for them. For instance, you might still have your twenty-six-year-old daughter's high school jacket—or the snowsuit your six-year-old son wore as a baby. Some of these items would best be stored in the attic. Baby clothing can be handled creatively by framing an outfit or two with baby pictures and hanging the display on a wall in your family room (or the family corner of the bagua in any other room).

 ESSENTIAL

If you truly have a lot of important stuff that you must keep but don't regularly use, consider off-site solutions. For a monthly rental fee, you can store everything from old tax records to small fishing boats. Of course, you may want to purchase insurance if you include such priceless objects as family heirlooms or antiques.

Hallways and Stairs: The Main Arteries of Chi

For hallways, the most common problem is that they are too narrow, which can be translated in feng shui as the symbol of a narrow mind. Open up the space with hall mirrors and a round crystal to reflect light and double the space. The crystal will also help get the chi flowing in many directions.

Hallways are definite clutter-magnets, because they are situated directly along the path of chi and attract clutter as it is brought into the home from outside sources. How many times have you gone to a garage sale, or a sale at a local department store, and come home with new things that looked really cool but for which you haven't quite found a place yet? Such wonderful little finds can quickly pile up in the hallway, as they await their final resting spot in your updated décor.

The way to curb clutter in the hallways is to make a rule that whatever comes into the home must immediately be put away. Also, if you can't visualize exactly where the new items will find their place in your home, then don't purchase them! There's nothing more wasteful than buying things you really don't need or want—and everything in feng shui needs to serve you somehow.

Like hallways, staircases are very important in feng shui because they represent the secondary "arteries" that carry energy throughout your home. If your door opens to a staircase that leads down a level, your positive chi will run down the steps; if it opens right to a staircase (as is often the case in apartments), you'll get too much negative chi at once. Place a small mirror on the outside of your front door to shield yourself from the rush of negative chi.

Clutter on staircases will also impede the flow of chi. What kinds of clutter typically accumulate on the steps? Shoes, books, clothes, and toys are common culprits. As these items begin their upward climb toward our bedrooms and attics, they leave a trail of clutter that represents unmade decisions about their worth. Are these things still meaningful to us, and if not, why are we leaving them in a place where they not only block chi, but also are on display for everyone who comes to our front door? Do you really want others to see that you haven't quite decided what to do with those ratty old tennis shoes that you keep around for God knows what reason?

 ESSENTIAL

Feng shui practitioners generally hate spiral staircases because their corkscrew shape accelerates chi as it passes through. If you have one of these staircases, place a small potted plant on one of the levels to slow down spiraling chi. Just don't overload the stairs, or you'll defeat the purpose!

Sometimes the design of a staircase can present unexpected obstacles for chi. If you have a staircase that appears challenging in any way, you can lessen the challenge by adding some visual elements like family pictures, décor items with a particular theme, or something that shows movement and progression. Using such accents will provide the mental message of "You can do it!" to anyone climbing your stairs.

Just be sure not to overdo your enthusiasm with too many "upward bound" photos or pictures, as they can have the opposite effect of slowing chi to a lingering stance on your stairs to absorb all of the excess energy. Chi needs freedom to climb to its highest potential in your home!

 ALERT

Disturbing the peace with "noise clutter" can be disruptive to chi. When you walk the path of chi through your home, be mindful of whether there's too much noise in the home—and do what you can to tone things down so that chi can do its healthy work.

Recycling Chi—and Clutter

Once it is free to roam to and through your home, chi circulates around it and then recycles itself for another round. This is a healthy, productive cycle in feng shui, and it is the ultimate goal as well. You have much to learn from this continuous cycle of chi. Like the recycling of chi, you, too, should be recycling the items you choose to have in your life. For each new item you purchase, you should try to give away another, particularly if it's one that's being intentionally replaced, such as a broken lawn mower or a too-small ladder. These kinds of things can be donated to charity if at all possible or else thrown away. The important thing is to make sure that you don't allow the new things to overpopulate your living space—crowding old, useless items into the crevices of your home and its immediate surroundings.

Recycling clutter in and especially around your home is a positive first step, but it takes discipline and more permanent solutions (such as fixed storage areas in closets or a garage or shed) to really stay on top of things. If you don't create lasting solutions to your clutter problems, you will still have lots of clutter and, as a result, lots of blocked chi. Clutter will continue to pile up even when you make regular attempts at clearing it.

Six Ways to Unblock Chi

As serious as it sounds, blocked chi can be dealt with effectively in several easy-to-implement ways. Here are six quick fixes:

Remove Obstacles

Deal with the clutter, and deal with it in long-lasting ways. Create permanent storage areas where your necessary items can live when they are not being used. If you feel chi is blocked somewhere, whether inside or outside of your home, it probably is and the situation needs to be remedied immediately.

Freshen Up

Cleaning a blocked room regularly will help prevent the "dust-magnet syndrome" from occurring. The less the clutter, the easier it will be to keep dust particles from covering the tops of all your furniture. But freshening up can go beyond cleaning—you can also freshen the air with some scented candles or incense.

Circulate the Air

When chi is stuck, the air seems thick and heavy; it doesn't appear to move freely throughout the room. You can get the air (and chi) circulating again by installing a small ceiling fan, hanging a wind chime, or opening windows where and when possible. Natural wind-movers are considered the best option in feng shui. Electrical alternatives are less desirable since their electrical force can interfere with the natural energy of chi.

Activate the Room

Sometimes, all a seemingly stagnant room needs is a little color and movement. Paint one or two walls a vibrant color, then add a movable hanging sculpture that dangles from your ceiling. This kind of change can literally get chi moving again in the room, unblocking it with a terrific new energy.

Add Life Forms

Plants and animals are fantastic chi-movers. Pets in particular can circulate chi throughout your home just by moving around, or by wagging a tail. This can help stuck chi to keep circulating in a more positive direction. Just be sure not to overdo it with too many plants or pets, as excess is never considered a good thing in feng shui.

Rearrange the Space

Often, as a last resort, you can completely rearrange the area where clutter seems to be blocking chi. This can help you gain a different perspective on the area, so that you can break yourself of the habit of dumping clutter there. This is especially helpful when there are other clutter-a-holics in your life who seem to be drawn to this particular space as a dumping ground.

You needn't make huge, sweeping modifications to the areas of your home where chi appears to be blocked. Feng shui consultants don't typically suggest such broad overhauls. Often, the smallest changes can be the most meaningful ones—and they can be just enough to make the difference in how you look at chi-inhibiting clutter.

Chapter 4

Adding Life to Your Living and Dining Rooms

The living room is a place where memories are made, and it's also where good memories are preserved. Call it "the museum of you" (and of your loved ones). From family pictures on the mantel to that fabulous ottoman you reupholstered yourself, your living room symbolizes the harmony you should have in every relationship, from family to community. These are the spaces most often shared by family and friends, and every element in them should be welcoming, as well as representative of who you are.

First Impressions

In many homes, the living room is the first room everyone sees upon entering through the front door. Ideally, it is visible from many areas of your home, as it is considered the "hub" of energy in feng shui. The "heart" of your home—a place that holds your memories and spreads joy into the rest of your living space throughout the house—the living room should be clearly visible or easily accessible from other rooms. The same can be true of your den, family room, or great room, especially if your home's layout doesn't feature a "formal" living room. Keep in mind that wherever these rooms are located in your home's blueprint, they have an inherent family energy and should be decorated or enhanced accordingly.

Surprisingly, the formal living room, in all its splendor, is often the one room in the home reserved for special occasions and visits from friends, family, and "company." Don't be one of those people like your Aunt Ida, who enshrines her living room furniture in sheets of protective plastic and constantly reminds you not to touch the "good" furniture. Good feng shui also means living life in flow with the Universe, and life is too short to spend hundreds of dollars decorating a living room that can't be lived in!

Room for Living

Your "room for living" should reflect who you are, and who you would like to see yourself become. It's a place for dreaming and introspection and connection with the self as well as for connection with others.

Incorporate your family traditions into your living room, too. This could simply mean that you watch football every Sunday in your living room, or that you have a weekly Friday-night movie "date" with your significant other. The important thing is to create a warm, welcoming, and "safe" place for you and other members of your family to come together to share your hopes, dreams, and ideas in a receptive, caring environment. That's what your living room is really all about.

 ALERT

> Like clutter, work can pile up quickly in your living room, so be sure to declare it off-limits in this important room for family gathering.

Use wisdom and power to enhance this meaningful room. First, you need to look at the direction the room is in. The best energies for a living room in feng shui come from the south, southeast, or southwest. These directions inspire creativity, lively conversation, and the positive exchange of ideas. West is also a good location for entertaining, so focus on that area of the room when having a party or get-together in your living room.

Position furniture so that it supports the main purpose of the room, which is to build a strong sense of family cohesiveness and community. That means you should have your sofa and chairs positioned so that they face the center of the room. Allow family and guests to choose their own best direction to sit, but be sure that no one is placed with their back to an entrance or window; if necessary, angle the piece of furniture so that your guest's back is protected by a corner or wall. You don't want your guests to feel open and vulnerable, right? Remember that your guests all need to be able to see an entrance to the room from where they are sitting, and you will be fine.

"Manifestation Central"

Not only is your living room a place for rest, relaxation, and community, it's also a space for creative visualization and manifestation. Here, you can dream your dreams—but you can also set them into action and bring them to fruition by adding specific elements to draw them into being.

 ESSENTIAL

If you want the help of your ancestors in an aspect of your life, place photos or objects that once belonged to them in that corner of a room. For example, to receive help in business, put their portraits in your wealth corner, as determined by using your bagua. Don't forget to say a daily prayer of thanks to your ancestors!

Balancing Act: The mixture of circles (round clock, mirror, and vase) and lines (the art deco and bamboo frames), as well as the mixture of metal, wood, and fire elements, brings a yin-yang balance to this mantel. Clutter would greatly upset this balance.

You can do your best to manifest the people or things you want to add to your life as long as your intention is focused on the highest good for all involved. Keep your intentions honest, pure, and of benefit to all, and you cannot go wrong.

Whether you want a new relationship (in which case, you should put pairs of things in the relationship corner of your living room) or a new job (in which case, you should activate the chi in the career section of your living room by hanging a crystal), know that you can affect change and make things happen simply by focusing your intention on a specific area of the bagua. Again, it's your manifestation tool!

 ESSENTIAL

If you've lost something that's important to you, consider placing a Chinese symbol of good luck in the last place you saw the item. A small, meaningfully placed statue of Quan Yin (the goddess of compassion) or Fu (the god of happiness and money luck) may help you "manifest" the missing item faster.

Clutter Hotspots in the Living Room

Some clutter is painfully obvious, like an overstuffed sofa crammed into a tiny corner of the room. But chi-blocking clutter can be found lurking in several other hiding spots:

- **Under coffee tables.** Here, it's most likely a pileup of books, magazines, and toys bringing chi to a grinding halt.
- **Along bookshelves or mantles.** Again, books are the primary culprit here. Other items of shelf clutter include bric-a-brac, too many framed photos, and mementos from long ago. These items might be better neatly stored in the attic "museum of the past."

- **Behind or under sofas or chairs.** Just as dust bunnies inexplicably seem to appear beneath your sofa, so it is with magazines, old picture frames, knitting/sewing kits, and other items put off for a rainy day. Does it ever really rain in your living room? Give away what used to be useful to you, but no longer has meaning.

- **Crammed into cabinets.** Remember that movie your entire family enjoyed—300 times—one summer, four years ago? Why is it still living in your entertainment center, behind thirty or forty other movies you no longer watch, and beside at least twenty-five CDs of music that no longer "sing" to you. Donate your old favorites to someone else who may not have experienced them and who can enjoy them for the first time.

Storage Solutions for Better Living

Because it is typically the most "lived-in" room of your home, your living room can experience an "energy pileup" faster than other rooms. But don't worry—there are many ways to stay on top of the situation.

- **Use a photo box or album.** Sort through old photos and put only a few choice ones in frames for display.

- **Cut and save interesting articles, not entire publications.** Or, purchase a magazine rack of metal or wood (both good balancing elements) to store only the most recent publications.

- **Keep the entertainment center closed when not in use.** This will limit electrical forces (a disruptive element) and enhance your family's communication.
- **Choose only what you currently love.** Get rid of old trinkets and mementos that have lost their meaning to you.
- **Organize using the bagua.** This is your mantra: "I will mindfully place only meaningful items in each area of this room." You can use this mantra for every room in your home, not just the living room.

It's important to recognize that you are not limited to these simple solutions for storage and removal of clutter in your living room. Experiment with several different methods, then choose the one that best seems to work within your own (and your family's) lifestyle. You may be surprised to find that all it takes to keep living room clutter from piling up is a simple sorting box kept close to the front door, giving your family a place to "plop" items before they even enter your sacred living space!

Space Constraints

What if your living room is tiny—or, shall we say, cozy? Here, the smallest amount of extraneous décor is sure to seem magnified, as even tiny groups of items can appear to engulf a room of 10 feet x 10 feet or less.

One solution is to decorate using only one or two striking, yet space-saving, pieces of furniture and a few well-chosen objets d'art.

If you have lots of interesting glasswork, photos, or meaningful objects, consider spreading the wealth and sharing them in other rooms of your home. You are never limited to the traditional in your decorating. Why not put a great sculpture in your bathroom, or a whimsical vase on your kitchen counter? Think "outside of the living room" for almost any décor item.

A final option is to refurbish your basement into a secondary living space—in the form of a finished recreation room. Here, you can have a less-formal space for entertaining your family and friends and more usable space throughout your home. This creative use of space allows even more positive chi to flow through your home, since people can carry it as they walk from room to room.

 ALERT

Don't forget that dust is clutter, too. Clean your living room on a weekly basis to keep the dust bunnies from populating in the space where your family shares its special times.

Smooth Soirees

The primary purpose of your living room is to be a place for the relaxation of yourself, your family, and any guests you may entertain from time to time. It can be a place of wonderful memories, but it is also your subconscious mind on display. Everything you place on the mantel, bookshelves, or coffee tables will be seen by all and perhaps interpreted by many.

 FACT

> The degree to which your living room is open, airy, and free of clutter shows the outside world that you honor your relationship with nature—and with them.

What does your living room clutter say about you? Mostly, it says you are stuck in the past, and unwilling or unready to move forward into your future. It could also indicate that you're trying to block changes from coming into your life, reflecting a deep insecurity or unwillingness to grow. Your guests will not perceive your living situation (and, worse yet, you) as healthy, even if they don't know about the principles of good feng shui.

Keeping the living room clear and open not only for your guests, but also for the future, will help complete your social circle in a healthy, positive way. When you have a party or soiree on your calendar, plan to clean up clutter one week before the event—and then perhaps again the day before, just to be on the safe side. No cheating—sliding old magazines under the couch may seem like a quick solution, but you'll pay for it in the end with feelings of guilt and oppression. If you're the least bit uncomfortable or preoccupied, your guests will definitely pick up on it and exit sooner to the comfort of their own homes. Don't miss out on an opportunity to shine in your clutter-free living room!

 ALERT

If you have a squabble or heated debate with others while in your living room, this is actually a form of emotional clutter. Do a space clearing to break up the negative energy; it can be as simple as ringing a bell or clapping your hands around the room.

Ditching "Dining Room Dump"

Because it is frequently located near the front door, the dining room can quickly become the "dumping ground" for all kinds of clutter-related items. It starts innocently enough, with a few books, papers, and pieces of mail placed on the dining room table for "just a little while." Days pass, and it's all still there because there is always something else that needs to be done. Before long, you've got a dining room dump of a mess.

The dining room is often an extension of your living room—it is where your family and guests spend time together in celebration and memory making. Dealing with clutter in your dining room is therefore as critical as it is in the living room, because these are the two rooms that symbolically show your face to the outside world.

When dealing with clutter in your dining room, there are a few obvious obstacles you could begin with.

What to Display—and What Not To

As lovely as collectibles are, these figurines can quickly overpopulate an entire room. Displaying a few of the better ones, and storing the rest will help. Add new interest to the room—make it a revolving exhibit. If they speak to you, keep them on display, but if they say more about you to others than you might feel comfortable with, store them in the attic or, better yet, give them away. Remember to be mindful and meaningful in the display of objects.

 ALERT

> Other people's clutter in your home can be just as oppressive to chi as your own array of junk. One visit to a clutter-free friend's home and you'll immediately notice the difference. If you're there with the clutter-a-holic you live with, point out the difference, but don't go home and clear their clutter for them. Instead, encourage and inspire them to do it themselves.

It is also important to be cautious of possible clutter when displaying your "good" silverware/dishes. By themselves, these are not clutter. But if you have too many of either, your sideboard or china closet will be overstocked—and before you know it, you'll have silverware everywhere in your dining room. Again, display a small and interesting grouping of things, and leave the rest in storage until you need them. Also remember that, despite their beauty, wine glasses are symbols of water and replenishment and should be kept in a closed china closet and protected from dust.

When creating a centerpiece for your dining room table, one lovely item, nicely centered in the middle of the table, is all you ever need. If you prefer fresh flowers, keep them healthy and alive—or pitch them. Dead or dying flowers represent negative energy in feng shui, and a table where you eat should be a place of health and vitality. Using a complementary table runner underneath the centerpiece will add softness and color.

Spiritual Displays

An increasing cultural interest in spirituality has led many people to create mini altars in areas such as their dining rooms. This is fine if kept clean (as in free of burnt incense remains) and clutter-free (as in a few meaningful spiritual reminders, like a statue of the Virgin Mary, an angel, or perhaps the goddess of mercy, Quan Yin). You'll be amazed at how focused your prayer sessions can be when you limit the number of deities represented in your altar!

Finally, think of the dining room's main purpose. It is for feeding your soul—and the souls of your friends and family. There's a reason most home designs instinctively place the dining room in the helpful people corner of the home's bagua. Contrary to the opulence and extravagance of kings and queens, don't make your dining room a shrine to excess. Respect yourself and your guests by keeping this room—and your living room—clean and clutter-free.

Once you've cleared the clutter in your living and dining rooms, think of how much better you'll feel about inviting others to your home. The best, and most liberating, part of this process is that it will allow you to say goodbye to those hurried, last-minute clutter-stuffing sessions in your closet or basement when you discover that company is on its way. But you'll also find that eliminating clutter by giving things away to others will increase your personal power of abundance—and you'll reap those benefits in many new and wonderful ways.

Chapter 5

The Clutter-Free Kitchen

If the entrance of your home is the mouth of chi, then your kitchen is definitely the stomach—and, just as the fortune cookie says, your stomach never lies. More and more, the kitchen is the room where both family and guests spend their time together. Like meals, though, some kitchens are nourishing and inviting, while others are too heavy and cause indigestion. Your uncluttered kitchen should be a center of health and efficiency.

Health and Balance

Good feng shui in the kitchen depends on many things, but most of the importance rests on harmony, balance, and mindfulness—both in design and practice. After all, the kitchen is the informal, yet critical center of your home, where everyone gathers to eat, talk, and plan for the future. It's where meals and dreams are often shared. The kitchen is the core source of your family's wealth, health, and prosperity, so it should be treated with the utmost reverence.

The ancient Chinese recognized this wisdom centuries ago, long before there was Williams-Sonoma, microwaves, or dishwashers. Westerners, in their ignorance of Eastern ways, at first considered feng shui in the kitchen to be a bit too "new agey." However, once its health and safety benefits were recognized, people began to adopt feng shui principles in the design and regular use of their kitchens. In fact, kitchen feng shui has come so far as an East-meets-West concept that it is regularly offered as a popular program through the National Kitchen & Bath Association. It's gone from being "ancient history" to a "hot trend"—in just a few thousand years!

The Feng-tional Kitchen

Although the following concept applies to all rooms, it bears repeating: You don't just start designing or redesigning your kitchen without clearing the clutter first. There's a modern feng shui saying that goes like this: "When you burp, you are full. Is your kitchen burping?"

Soulful Kitchen: A kitchen that's free of clutter is the epitome of healthy digestion.

Your kitchen will "burp" (or seem like it needs to) if the drawers and cupboards are full of things you no longer use or need. As an experiment, one person actually went through each cabinet and her pantry and put all the food she wasn't using into a huge pile. By the end of the day, there was enough food to feed a family of four for two weeks—and that was just the food that the woman didn't like!

Clean out your cupboards, donate food you don't want to homeless shelters, and pitch the things you don't need anymore. You'll be surprised how much lighter this will make you feel, and how much it will contribute to your prosperity when you give up the need to hoard.

Kitchen Clutter Zones

There are several clutter zones in the kitchen. This is not surprising; since the kitchen is the room most frequented by everyone in your family, it can easily become the great dumping ground in your home.

Do you have a difficult time finding anything in your kitchen? Are things never where you think they should be? If so, you could have a widespread problem with clutter in your kitchen. More specifically, your clutter could have blocked the chi in one of several problem areas found in many kitchens.

Kitchen countertops and surfaces can easily become a clutter problem. Countertops full of utensils, storage bins, coupons, recipe books, and more may affect you negatively when you are ready to prepare a good meal. Do you notice that you feel differently when the whole counter is clear and clean?

Garbage bins, although they are a necessity, undoubtedly create clutter. Trash is not only unsightly, but it is also an energy-zapper. Bins that are filled to the brim and overflowing are unhealthy, but they also keep a lid on your chi. Try to empty trash once a day—and store kitchen garbage in concealing cabinetry. This will also keep your cat or dog out of the trash!

Speaking of cabinets, be careful not to stuff them to the point where they won't even close. The cabinets directly under the sink are often the most overcrowded; ironically, this is where many people store their cleaning supplies. At least once per month, you should do a clearing of all items that are expired or no longer needed; regular purging can make your kitchen come alive with energy.

Although every kitchen needs appliances, it is possible to create less clutter out of them. Keep larger appliances clean and in good working order. Don't store a lot of items (such as gadgets and knickknacks) on your stovetop—this will hold down the positive energy of your cooking, and could make you feel too oppressed to cook at all. Limit the magnetic energy on your refrigerator with a few interesting magnets versus an entire menagerie. With smaller appliances, replace them if they are not in good working order, and try to store them in cupboards where they can be protected from dust or dirt.

 ALERT

> Chi can be slowed in its progress by a crowded kitchen. Shelves that are crowded and floors with stacks of clutter can impede or even stop the flow of chi. Keep a clear path at all times.

Floors can easily become a clutter nightmare. If you have to carve a path to get from one end of your kitchen to the other, you have a serious clutter problem on your kitchen floor. If you keep items such as bottles, cans, or newspapers for recycling, consider a special storage bin for these in your garage versus your kitchen. The kitchen is a place for life, health, and sustenance—not the oppressive energy of things associated with the past (e.g., empty cans, old newspapers, etc.). One way to add life to your kitchen is to place a fresh potted plant in the health corner of your kitchen. Just remember to feed it and keep it healthy!

Storage and Cleaning Solutions

If space is truly limited in your kitchen, a kitchen cart or extra shelving can offer opportunity for more sensible storage options. A cart or shelf can hold several canisters full of cooking supplies, ingredients, small appliances, and even bottles of wine. A bowl full of fresh fruit centered on a kitchen cart can be a warm, inviting, and healthy touch.

 ESSENTIAL

> To cultivate good chi, you must harmonize the five elements in your kitchen: wood, fire, earth, metal, and water.

Remember, it's not only what you keep, it's how you keep it that counts.

Keep your kitchen clean because it represents prosperity in the form of good health and wealth. Dirty dishes, stoves, and refrigerators can block your abundance in these important aspects of your life, and they can also cause digestive problems in your body. Dirt can "clog" the arteries of your soul, making you feel unhealthy physically *and* emotionally.

Food should be stored away when not being used for cooking. You should use metal or wood canisters to store bread, flour, and sugar, especially if your storage canisters will be located between the stove and the refrigerator. This will balance your elements of fire (stove) and water (fridge) with a little wood and metal in between.

Speaking of refrigerators, you can also apply the principles of good feng shui to the inside of your cold food storage. Use the bagua to determine which foods best correspond with each element—or simply go by the usefulness factor. If you sort food by its usefulness to you and your family, you will always keep the things you need within close reach, and you will begin to practice the kind of mindfulness that helps you instinctively remove the things you don't need or use.

Practicing mindfulness will make a huge difference in lightening your mind and your body. You will store only the foods you know you'll use, effectively eliminating the kind of refrigerator clutter that makes people pack on extra pounds out of boredom.

A "feng-tional" kitchen will invigorate and nourish all the inhabitants of your home.

 ESSENTIAL

To be truly "feng-tional," a kitchen must allow the maximum amount of good chi, neither stagnant nor rushing, to pass through it.

Cooking Up Good Chi: The Fundamentals

The kitchen is the hearth and heart of your home, and it's especially important for that room to have good chi. Following is a helpful checklist:

- **Eliminate clutter.** Throw away what you can't use; donate or recycle what will serve others.
- **Keep your kitchen clean.** Since it represents prosperity in the form of good health and wealth, a kitchen should be consistently kept clean.
- **Maintain good ventilation.** To allow the maximum amount of good chi to pass freely through your kitchen, open windows and doors to invigorate and nourish all of the inhabitants of your home.
- **Use good lighting.** Proper lighting is very important; overhead, full-spectrum lighting is best.
- **Choose good colors.** Earth colors (like forest green, which is associated with growth), balanced with bright white, work best in kitchens.
- **Include ancestors in the family dining experience.** Bring your heritage to the table through photos, recipes, or a place at the table, and give thanks to the Universe for every meal so that you will continue to be so blessed.

As you continue to use feng shui, certain practices will become habit. Occasionally review the list, however, to remind yourself of your intentions, and refocus your energies where needed.

Optimizing Nutritious Chi

So, when it comes time to prepare a meal, what else can you do to cook up some deliciously good chi in your kitchen? Here are some suggestions:

Purchase the Freshest Ingredients

Heavily processed food has stagnant chi, while fresh foods offer vitality and life-giving energy.

You should also buy only what you will use. This applies to food, but it especially applies to kitchen appliances and equipment. Don't buy a bread maker, high-speed blender, juicer, or other specialized gadget unless you plan to be using it often. Waste is bad feng shui, because it represents wasted wealth.

Balance Your Meat and Vegetables

Limit your meat intake, and be sure your meals include fresh vegetables. Meat alone is too yang and can upset your stomach, as well as contribute to heart disease. Meat represents life taken away, while vegetables offer restoration. Chalk up a point for vegetarianism!

Do a Quick Meditation

Before you start to prepare food, take a deep purifying breath, relax, and focus on the task at hand. You are creating nourishing food that will help your body (and your family's bodies) to grow. You are a giver of life, so take a moment to give thanks to the Universe for providing the great food you are about to cook and serve. Make sure you are cooking with good intention, and don't cook if you are in a bad mood. You should always be relaxed and focused.

Set the Mood

Before you start to cook, you may want to put on your favorite feng shui CD, pour a glass of your favorite beverage, light a candle or two, and go to it. Before you know it, there's a nice dinner to go with the music and candles. Don't wait for special occasions—every day you can eat dinner with your entire family is a special occasion. Do whatever you can to create comfort in your kitchen. You'll keep excess weight off if you create comfort rather than eat it!

Check Your Feng Shui

While you are cooking, do a quick feng shui assessment. Is everything cleaned up the way it should be? Are you amassing clutter as you cook? If so, clear it away as soon as you can. Yes, that means that you will begin cleanup as soon as you begin cooking! Store your trash out of sight, either under the sink, in a pantry, or in another room. Rinse dishes, especially if you know that you won't get around to cleaning them right away. Keep extra composting bags handy to put food scraps in before, during, and after your meal. You won't want to put these in the trash, since they will start to decompose and smell quickly. Bad smells equal bad chi!

The Yin-Yang of Eating

In Chinese thinking, you literally are what you eat. If you eat lots of hot and spicy foods, you are eating more yang than yin. If you eat lots of foods that are grown underground, from the earth, you are eating more yin foods. Neither is bad for you, but you should always strive for balance with your own internal chi.

Be mindful of what you are eating. In other words, if you are feeling a little on the lethargic side, try eating more yang foods to counteract that feeling. If you're a little agitated, a yin food—one that grows outside in the sun and fresh air, like tea—can also work to calm you down. The feng shui art of balance applies to your insides as well as your surroundings!

While you can't arrange your food neatly within the bagua of your stomach, you *can* control what goes in and why. This takes you back to the practice of mindfulness, of thinking about what you do and putting purpose behind every action. You are literally practicing good feng shui inside your own body if you listen to its cues—if you are mindful without being "stomach-ful."

 ESSENTIAL

Arrange time-sensitive foods so that they remain in the forefront of your pantry or refrigerator. This way, you aren't likely to forget about them—leaving them in the "food museum" long after their time.

Stomach Clutter: Cures for Overindulgence

You know the syndrome: You're at the grocery store, and you're hungry. You push your cart up and down each aisle, barely glancing at the careful list you prepared before your trip. When you return home, you have more food in your cupboards than ever—and soon, more in your stomach than you had originally planned.

Or perhaps you've gone out for dinner, and you've ordered way more than your stomach can handle. You could feel obligated to overindulge, especially if someone else is paying for the meal.

How can you be sure you're suffering from "stomach clutter"? Symptoms such as stomach upset/indigestion, acid reflux, and weight gain are obvious physical signs of stomach clutter. But there can also be signs of overindulgence in your pantry, such as boxes with contents half-eaten months ago and mega-size boxes of snacks everywhere.

Decluttering your stomach can be simple, as well as quickly rewarding for your body, mind, and spirit. You can cut back on the culinary clutter by doing the following:

- **Eliminate unhealthy munchies.** Cut back on the greasy potato chips, salty pretzels, and sugar-filled candies. Keep healthier foods such as granola, raisins, yogurt, and fruit more readily available.
- **Exercise more.** The more energy you burn, the more likely you'll be inclined to replace that energy

with healthy fuel (e.g., fiber, fresh fruits, and fresh vegetables).

- **Cut back.** Don't try to eat more than you feel like consuming just because it's there, especially when eating out. Eat half and take the other half home for later in the week.
- **Drink more water.** In feng shui, when you need balance, you look to nature. Water is a cleansing force in nature; it cleanses and clears your body of all impurities.
- **Consider a "leftovers night."** To purge your refrigerator on a regular basis, designate one night per week as a smorgasbord of leftovers.
- **Look within for the cause.** Stress is a major driver of stomach clutter; emotional eating is the most common cause of stomach trouble among adults. Other causes include: worry over not having enough, unhealthy habits of other family members, and addictions to unhealthy foods.

The most important thing you can do to control clutter in your body—and the more symbolic body of your kitchen—is to find better ways of dealing with the issues behind the clutter. Understanding the psychology behind kitchen and stomach clutter will ultimately prove your best defense against negative gastronomical consequences.

Chapter 6

Clutter Above, Clutter Below: Attics and Basements

In medicine, the saying "As above, so below" means that the thoughts and attitudes in your mind help to determine the potential for good health or illness of your body below. Similarly, what you find on top of your house is a strong indicator of what you'll find below. Is your attic stuffed with musty books and clothes, and sundry relics of the past? Then it's a good bet that your basement is as well.

From Top to Bottom

In feng shui, the basement is viewed as your foundation and the attic as your potential. Effectively, you are impinging on your support and threatening your potential, not to mention disrupting the flow of chi, when you use your attic and basement as warehouses for a myriad of junk.

Not all of it is "junk," of course, as you will discover the minute you inform your family members that you are thinking of discarding some of it. Still, it may as well be if it is not kept in good order or easily located if and when you actually choose to do so. If you cannot even set foot in your attic or basement without immediately stepping over some item, or if you cannot find a comfortable place to sit and easily investigate what you have or remember what that might be, then you know that those spaces are in serious need of decluttering.

Hoarding Hotspots

For many people, the basement and attic are the places of indecision—meaning that they are where we store all the things we cannot figure out what else to do with. These are the things like the kids' baby toys about which Mom is sentimental, or old sporting equipment Dad is unable to part with, even though he hasn't played softball or bocce in fifteen years.

Here you'll also find all the gifts from friends and relatives that we never really liked or used but which we cannot bring ourselves to give away, just in case the giver should visit and expect to see it on display. Or, worst of all, they might by a stroke of supernaturally bad luck find out that we have gotten rid of it. ("Look, George—isn't that painting in the junk store window the 'Pigs with Wings' that we gave Albert and Alice for their wedding twenty years ago!") That's certainly a likely scenario and a good reason for keeping such items somewhere in the house for the rest of our lives, isn't it? Many women can tell the familiar story of gathering up a heap of their husband's old clothing and putting it in bags for charity, only to have their husbands rifle through those bags, allegedly "out of curiosity," and ultimately leave only a T-shirt or stained hat behind for the needy. Or of gathering up children's toys from those same places for the same purpose, only to have their children whine that they have to have said toys and, in fact, really have been "looking" for them for ages!

As if your own junk wasn't enough, there's another potential problem: local garage sales that attract family members like moths to a flame. They cannot wait to purchase the junk from other people's basements and attics, and it is only a matter of time before much of this stuff ends up in yours. Sometimes, it seems that neighbors are only swapping each other's junk and perhaps should save themselves the time and trouble of setting up yard and garage sales and simply collect all their unwanted stuff and automatically deposit it on each other's doorsteps.

Letting Go

It is bad enough that we spend our money on items that we don't use or wear. But rather than acknowledging our mistakes, we compound them by hanging on to these items, making space for them in our homes and psyches, and allowing them to weigh us down from above or pull us down from below. We need, instead, to be freeing ourselves from excess baggage so that we can make space in our lives for the new and the wonderful—for what we really need and truly will use. And we have to be firm in our resolve to clean and clear and actually dispose of or donate those items that haven't seen the light of day in ages and for a very good reason. As with relationships we have shed in the past, these things may look good in hindsight, but when you closely examine them without the rose-colored glasses, you see that, like those old relationships, the love of these things ended for very good reasons.

The junk in your attic and basement—and this does not refer to old family photos or other memorabilia of actual value to you financially or nostalgically, but the honest-to-goodness *junk*—needs to go, and the sooner the better. The best proof of this may be if you are reading this chapter, seeing yourself in it, and feeling guilty that you haven't done what you know you need to do. Think of this chapter as your affirmation—your emotional support in helping to give you the strength you will need, the courage of your convictions, in finally, for once and for all, tackling those piles of unused, unwanted things in your attic and basement and freeing yourself from them forever! This is your battle cry, your Declaration of Independence. Repeat the following, "I (your name) WILL dispose of the items in my basement and attic that I no longer use or have any intention of using ever again!" There. Feel better? Now, let's look at the problem in greater detail.

Your Highest Potential

We tend to use the concept of height positively—we speak of our "higher selves" or "higher purpose"; we talk of those who are "higher ups"; we say that we want to "climb higher" in our jobs or in our lives; and, of course, spiritually, we look up, or heavenward. In Victorian times, new babies were walked up to the attic in a symbolic act suggesting that the child would go far in life.

Now, imagine yourself with X-ray vision, standing on one of the lower floors of your home, casting your eyes upward toward your attic. Does what you see in there really fit these images? How high does your potential seem as you envision the dusty disco clothing from the '70s, the warped Vanilla Fudge and T-Rex albums, the velvet "Poker-Playing Dogs" artwork, and the lopsided pottery that you made in your college art class? In fact, precisely which items can you "see" as you gaze into your attic that can be said to fit into this picture of the sublime? If you can think of even one or two, then these are keepers. But if all you can see are relics of your past that are better kept out of sight, or useless items that were never even "once used and enjoyed" but instead went straight to the attic—some still in their original boxes and wrapping paper—then you know what you must do.

Those items that you decide to keep must be sorted, organized, and properly stored to prevent mildew, yellowing, and other signs of deterioration. Special photos, jewelry, and wardrobe boxes should be used.

 FACT

> Old newspaper articles should be laminated for preservation, and photos, if not in special photo boxes, should be labeled as best as possible and placed in photo albums.

Depending on the type of attic you have, perhaps a bookshelf or two might be appropriate for storing old books that you cannot bear to toss or give away, but that you don't necessarily want downstairs with your others.

If yours is a walk-in attic, then try to set it up as you would other rooms, with an eye toward letting the energy flow through freely. You have probably boxed your various holiday decorations but perhaps have made no effort to organize the sports equipment, toys, or old school projects. Always have a large garbage bag or two when you go to your attic and think, "What can I toss or donate to charity? What in here do I truly need or want to hang onto, and what is here that I have not used in a long time and have no intention of using any time soon?" Be ruthless and as unsentimental as you can, or that pile will not shrink.

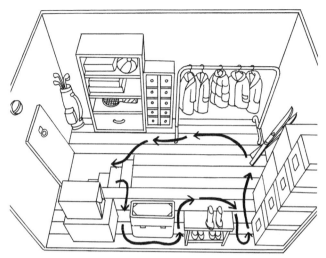

The Good-Chi Attic: Clutter is just as neatly stored in this healthy attic as in a well-planned closet. Note that you can use coatracks to store clothes in addition to boxes.

Discovering What's Worth Keeping

Always keep in mind that, as the years pass, you will be adding to what is already there. Is there any room for more? If not, have you taken a vow never to add to your current collection? It may help you, if you are not planning to move in the near future, to imagine that you are. What items in your attic would you actually pack up and move with you? All the items that you wouldn't be willing to take with you then should probably be gotten rid of now. Why wait?

ESSENTIAL

If you are storing empty boxes, keep just a few, and fold them so they will stack or lean against a wall and take up much less room.

If you can bear it, try to unburden yourself of old school papers, old love letters and other mementos of former relationships, and similar kinds of keepsakes that can prevent you from moving forward in life. You will find that once you have disposed of many of these remnants of your distant past, you will feel lighter and freer to face the future. Perhaps you could start by choosing a few of the more significant items to keep while tossing or giving away the rest. Then, later, you may feel up to getting rid of these, as well. You always can take the decluttering process in small stages.

A Strong Foundation

Sometimes, when we're feeling low or down on ourselves, we'll say that our self-esteem or our feelings are "in the basement." We even use that phrase to say where our financial investments are. In this sense, "the basement" means the lowest point, and it's considered a pejorative term. However, in feng shui terms, your home's basement is your foundation or starting point, the place from which you derive strength and the point from which you grow upward and outward. The basement does not have to be a dark, dingy place in which all of our unwanted belongings are stored. Many of us use our basements as offices and dens, as play areas for our children, as another useful room in the house. Even then, however, much of our "stuff" is stored in the depths of our homes.

First Get Organized

As with the attic, you should organize your belongings in your basement. Just the very process of organizing will bring you back into contact with many items that you had forgotten you ever had. And if that is the case, perhaps it is high time to dispose of or give away those items. Also, as with the attic, you should be asking yourself what, if any, of this accumulation serves a useful purpose in your life. Then ask what items easily could disappear from your life without being missed.

Undoubtedly, the items that you learn to your surprise that you still own could be good candidates for the trash or the box for charity. If you want, you also could assess these items in the basement, as well as in the attic, for what they could bring you monetarily. If you sold the usable items to individuals or secondhand shops, you would not only be clearing space in your life but also making some money to finance your future.

Basement Storage Solutions

Don't forget that your basement has some walls, and you could put up hooks and shelving. Utility shelves are also inexpensive and can hold a number of items, including canned and boxed food. If you don't have a pantry in your kitchen, or if you need a place to stash the overflow or allow for "just-in-case" on stormy days when you can't get out of the house, shelves in the basement are perfect. Now that discount stores are so popular, including the large shopping clubs in which items are sold in bulk, there is nothing better than well-organized, contained basement space to store the extras.

If you do find yourself stocking up on canned and dried foods because of all the great bulk food sales and weekly specials at the grocery store, you also may find that you have overdone it. Fifteen cans of tomatoes and another ten of corn and beans, along with multiples of other products, can make your basement look like a fallout shelter or a soup kitchen. It might be advisable to get out the cookbooks and look up some good, one-dish recipes, such as soups and stews that will use several types of canned vegetables and dried pasta.

 ESSENTIAL

> You might want to cut back on your grocery shopping for a week or two, especially on fresh produce, in order to consume some of the perishable products and clear your shelves. Or, you might want to donate many of the canned goods to a local homeless shelter or food bank.

Storage containers are one of the items you might consider buying in one of these super discount stores.

So much of what is lying around loose in your basement, taking up extra space, can be stored neatly in plastic, transparent storage boxes. Not only will they then be kept out of the way, but you will also be able to see at a glance what is in the boxes.

The Junk That Must Go

No matter what else you do, be sure to discard the junk—the broken, the torn, and the outdated. Phonebooks and almanacs from ten years ago, old magazines, and ancient financial and property information for accounts and items you no longer have are really good places to start. Decks of cards with fewer than fifty-two cards and board games with missing pieces are another. Broken or never-used exercise equipment can go next. If you start by eliminating these kinds of items, you will find yourself "on a roll," and moving on to the other, more difficult items that need organizing or discarding but take a little more thought. Many can be recycled and given a new life outside of the confines of your basement or attic. Set such items free!

Keeping Useful Items Handy

Clean out those old cans of paint and jars of paint thinner. Check with your city government to learn the proper way of disposing of such toxic items. Generally speaking, you are not permitted to dump these down the drain because they can pollute the public water supply. If you keep tools in your basement, put them in toolboxes and keep them on shelves so that you can find what you want, when you want it. There are few situations more frustrating than having something break and not being able to fix it easily because you can't put your hands on the right tools quickly.

Organize nails and screws by type and size so that you're not rooting around in those containers when you need something. Especially helpful are items like multi-head screwdrivers in which the heads are all stored in the handle, thereby keeping everything in one place and eliminating the need to store multiple screwdrivers in your toolbox. While you're organizing, make sure that you have and can easily find basic items, like hammers, pliers, and measuring tape.

 FACT

> One good storage solution is a plastic bag holder, shaped like a windsock that hangs from a wall hook. Bags go in the top and can be pulled out from the bottom, one at a time. Paper bags can be kept folded up, nesting one inside the other, in a wire rack or basket hanging on the wall.

We often store our cleaning implements, like mops, brooms, scrub brushes, pails, and appliances such as shop vacuums and steam cleaners in our basements, as well. Try to keep these items together, and, whenever possible, have wall hooks for the mops, brooms, and pails so that they are off the floors. Most of these cleaning tools will have holes in the handles for that purpose.

A Family Project

Suffice it to say that few of us finish a major basement clearing in one day. Take several days, if needed, so long as you are making some progress. You might want to organize according to what piece of the project you will tackle on which day. And don't go it alone if you don't have to. Get your entire family to help. The more vested they are in the outcome, the more likely they will be to help you keep the basement in good shape after you have finished cleaning and organizing.

Keep in mind that starting with something simple, like throwing away the obviously outdated or damaged items, and also those items you can't identify, often gives us the incentive we need to continue. As we start seeing improvement, even our smallest victory, such as a full trashcan or two by the end of the day, we want to enlarge upon it. As we continue, the space clears, the chi flows, and our foundation is strengthened.

It All Comes Out in the Wash

In many homes, the laundry area is in the basement. Ironically, although this is an area associated with cleanliness, it can become, like the rest of the basement, disorganized and filled with junk: half-filled detergent boxes or bottles that we have decided we no longer want; old clothes that were washed and hung to dry long ago but have been forgotten; rocks and toys and other items that were emptied from children's pockets or found in the washer or dryer months ago; single, lonely socks; and large items, such as blankets and pillows, that need washing but seem too cumbersome to do "right now." Not to mention, where there is space, the overflow from the rest of the basement. Sometimes, there is barely room to stand, and the table for folded laundry is so full of other items, it is unusable. We feel uncomfortable in this space, and doing laundry, already a dreaded task, becomes even more of a chore than ever.

 ESSENTIAL

If you are so inclined, try to clear enough space for an ironing board as well. Even with all of the new, wrinkle-resistant fabrics, many people still enjoy wearing cotton and other fabrics that require occasional light pressing. Keep your iron in good, working order, and every now and then, change your spray bottles to keep them, and your clothes, fresh.

Do yourself a favor and take the time to really clear out this space. Most of what is here and is not being used specifically for washing and drying should be tossed out. Put in extra shelving, if there is room, or drying lines and racks for sweaters and delicates. Create some space in which to stand, bend, fold, and reach.

Overhead cabinets may be another possibility, with doors to hide some of the detergents, stain removers, dryer sheet boxes, and so forth. If you have a utility sink in the basement, keep it clean and clear of clutter as well, and be sure to keep clean towels and bars of soap and scrub brushes to remove stubborn paint and grease from dirty hands after a messy home-improvement project.

Finishing the Job

Just because you have a small space, tucked away under the stairs, or an attic that is not a room but more a storage place among the rafters, doesn't mean you should leave all manner of unused, unwanted "stuff" in those places. Whether they are officially rooms or not, having those areas full to overflowing with junk and pieces of your past still inhibits chi, not to mention prevents you from using that space more wisely. Not every space needs to be filled, it should be noted. Free flow of energy through open space is best of all. When was the last time you grabbed a flashlight and really investigated what was in those unlivable spaces where we tend to shove things inside and shut the door? Above and below, potential and foundation, tall space or crawl space—all should be cleaned, sorted, and, wherever possible, freed of junk and the weight of the past.

Now that you have tackled your attic, basement, and other storage areas, you have also created a safe haven for memories and for your dreams and aspirations. The feeling of accomplishment after such a major undertaking is intense. Best of all, any other areas that need cleaning and organizing will pale in comparison because few other areas retain such an abundance of old and unused items. We banish those items to those upper and lower, hidden-away spaces, and when we have liberated ourselves from those things, we make room for all kinds of possibilities. We feel renewed and invigorated. Be sure to take some time to bask in the glow of your accomplishment—and to enjoy the tax break for your charitable donations or the mad money from your yard sale!

By having both your attic and your basement shipshape, you are achieving balance. "As above, so below," like the balancing of female yin and male yang energy, is so critical in the philosophy of feng shui. You want to feel centered and grounded in your home, and the space clearings that you have worked so hard to complete will help you achieve this goal.

Chapter 7

More Peaceful Nights

Do you remember those long nights when you were small, when you couldn't sleep because you just knew there were monsters lurking under your bed? Now, the monsters are in the clutter under your bed, atop your dresser, and in your closet. They may not be as scary as the bogeymen of your childhood, but these monsters can prevent the flow of healing energy that you need in order to enjoy all the benefits that flow from a good night's sleep.

Placement of Your Bedroom

Unless you built your home from scratch, you obviously did not have anything to do with where your bedroom was placed. Chances are that when you bought or rented your home, you didn't think about feng shui or even know much about it. The questions of which direction the bedroom faces in and where it is in relation to other rooms or doors or bathrooms did not concern you. If, after you learn a bit more about ideal placement, these aspects do begin to concern you, don't lose sleep over it! No matter what your bedroom situation is, there is usually a remedy that will allow you to get a restful night's sleep.

Sleep Tight

Contrary to what many people think, a small room is best for sleeping, because the energy is contained (just as long as the room is not filled with clutter). The best location for your room is far away from the front door of your home, where so much energy flows through.

If insomnia is a problem for you, "west is best" for the direction in which you should face, because that's where the sun sets. However, if you find it easy to fall asleep but difficult to wake up, try facing east. The direction of the sun, rising or setting, will help you determine what works best for you. Room color can help offset too much or too little sunlight, as well.

Tossing and Turning

If you slip into dreamland almost as soon as your head hits the pillow, you probably can move on to another section of this book. But if you're having trouble finding a smooth transition from wakefulness to dreamland, it could be because your bedroom feng shui is closer to a nightmare than a dream.

First of all: Get rid of the clutter! Having remnants of your day, your work, and other aspects of your wakeful life scattered about your floor, hiding under your bed, and covering the surfaces of your dresser and any other furnishings impedes chi and your sleep.

Try not to sleep directly under the bathroom on a floor above you. Being close to plumbing tends to drain chi.

Have calm, soothing colors on your walls, floor, and furnishings—and keep electronics out of the bedroom as much as possible to avoid the constant flow of energetic electrical current while you're trying to catch some ZZZs.

Put only soft, comfortable sheets and blankets on your bed, and avoid using dead animal skins. No bearskin rugs on the floor! Dead animals in a room are very bad for chi.

Keep your work area in another room, or cover it up when you sleep. Work and sleep just don't mix—and you don't want one of those frustrating dreams in which you're at work, only to wake up from your restless sleep and actually be there already!

Rest Easy

Safety and privacy in your bedroom are important to restful sleep, too. A bedroom that is too open to the rest of the house may be disquieting. If you must sleep in a space that otherwise lacks privacy, such as a living room, you should try to define the sleeping area clearly and protect it with a piece of furniture such as a bookcase or perhaps a tall screen.

Remember, too, that your bedroom should offer a contrast to your hectic, daily life.

Mirror, Mirror . . .

Your bedroom should reflect your personal style, but mirrors should not reflect you—or you and your partner—in your bedroom. Mirrors displace the energy in your room, affecting your sleep, and even could draw a third party into your romantic relationship. Mirrors over the bed are especially bad for that reason!

For one thing, you might be startled by your own movements in a mirror if you should get up in the middle of the night. It's also thought that each night, as we sleep, our souls travel through space and time. As they begin their journey, they, too, may be jarred by reflections in a mirror, including those of anything that is less than aesthetically pleasing in the room.

 ESSENTIAL

The advantages of mirrors in interior decorating—opening up space and making a room appear larger and brighter—are serious disadvantages in the bedroom for those very reasons.

A mirror opposite the door of your bedroom is a bad idea, too, because it will reflect energy back toward the entrance, interrupting the energy flow of your room. Exceptions to the no-mirrors rule are:

- If you cannot avoid having your back to the door, then a mirror on the opposite wall allows you to see anyone coming into your room. But use only one mirror, preferably circular, which facilitates a blending of energies.
- If your bed is directly under ceiling beams or a sloping ceiling, which disrupts or suppresses energy flow, then a mirror facing upward can help.
- If you have scenery outside your bedroom, you use a mirror to reflect it inward.

If you cannot simply remove the mirrors in your bedroom, you might consider covering them, such as with drapery or fabric art. If you do so, though, remember to use fabric of a muted shade because bright colors are stimulating and can disturb your sleep.

Bedtime or Bedlam?

Where should your bed be? Let's first talk about where it should *not* be. Your bed should not be facing a doorway, with the foot of the bed toward the door. This is viewed as the death position in many cultures and is highly unlucky. Your bed should also not be aligned with the door because you should be able to see anyone coming through the doorway. Also, this parallel position will create a disruption in energy flow that could disturb your sleep.

 ALERT

> Placing your bed against a window is not a good idea either, since the chi will flow too quickly out of the room.

Another inauspicious location for a bed is under a beam, sloping ceiling, ceiling fan, bright light, or overhanging shelf or cupboard. All of these things disturb or suppress energy flow. Don't put your mattress on the floor, either, because that causes disturbed sleep and will literally hold you down from achieving your dreams. In your bedroom, you should seek to elevate yourself!

If possible, you should not sleep on a bed that was owned by someone else. Beds absorb a person's energy, and chances are that you do not know whether the energy of the previous owner was good.

Don't sleep in a metal-framed bed. Not only is metal cold, it will also enhance the electromagnetic energy of electrical appliances in your home, which could prevent a restful night's sleep. Speaking of currents, unplug as many of your electrical appliances in your room at night as you can to cut off the constant flow of electricity through the wiring.

Don't sleep in a room directly below a toilet on the floor above, and if there is no door between your bedroom and bathroom, use something to separate the rooms. Bathrooms are believed to be "draining," literally, of your energy.

If you are part of a couple and you value your relationship, it's recommended that you not sleep in a king-sized bed, which is too large and can have the same effect as sleeping separately.

Some more tips: You should have a solid headboard (but not one shaped like a headstone). Use a canopy to separate your bed from what's over it if your bed is under a sloping ceiling, structural beam, or toilet on the floor above. Place the bed diagonally opposite the doorway to your bedroom, in a corner, so that you will see the door without directly facing it. Being able to see the doorway provides added security, which facilitates sleep. The idea is to be out of alignment with the energy flowing through the doorway while still keeping the doorway in sight.

The Clutter Monster in the Bedroom

Many people have a tendency to allow their bedrooms to become filled with stuff. They rationalize that any guests who visit them will be highly unlikely to see their bedrooms, so why not throw all of those old boxes and magazines underneath the bed? It's that kind of thinking that can keep you up at night!

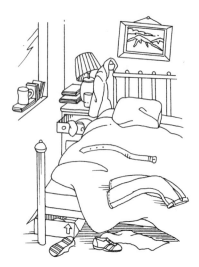

Bed Unrest: Clutter on, under, and around your bed can make for restless nights—don't sleep on unmade decisions like these.

For the best possible energy flow and a good night's sleep, you really do want a room that is free of clutter. For instance, clothing that retains energy from your daily life should be put away. The space under your bed should be just that—space: no storage boxes or fuzzy bedroom slippers, no snack food or dishes. No clutter of any kind. Also, except for the reasons noted earlier, there should be no mirrors in your bedroom, and few, if any, knickknacks. No electrical appliances, including television sets, radios, stereos, computers, hair curling sets, or hair dryers. No exercise equipment, and absolutely no work desk!

Try to reduce the amount of *things* you have, from the menagerie of glass animals to the jungle of real or artificial plants. In fact, living plants in your room at night are a bad idea, anyway. Nighttime is when plants give off carbon dioxide and take in oxygen, just the reverse of the process during the daytime.

 ESSENTIAL

> If you must have a workspace (like a desk or computer) in your bedroom, just be sure to cover the work area at night, especially any electrical items such as your computer.

Too many pictures on the walls, piles of books and magazines on the chairs and floor, and similar clutter will block the flow of natural energy and prevent you from achieving the best possible night's sleep. Even very large bedrooms should be sparsely furnished. Don't feel compelled to fill every inch of space, unless you truly enjoy insomnia.

Eliminating clutter doesn't mean you have to eliminate the things you enjoy. Instead of banishing books from your bedroom, find a way to accommodate them and enhance the energy flow that induces sleep. Just place a pyramid-shaped bookcase in the wisdom corner of your bedroom. The books will be much more neatly arranged, and the shelf's pyramid shape works nicely because it is an ancient symbol of higher knowledge.

Watch Your Tone

First and foremost, your bedroom is a place to rest your body, mind, and spirit. Be mindful of your decorative elements and their sensory impact. Calm colors, soothing fabrics, and subdued lighting will help you release the stresses of your day and prepare you for the sleep your body needs.

Color Me Sleepy

Colors can do a lot to enhance your bedroom, but they can cause disturbance, too. Be especially color conscious if you have difficulty sleeping. For instance, bright red is a great color for a fire engine, but not for your bedroom. Just as it startles and wakes up drivers and pedestrians, who rightly associate the color with emergencies and adrenaline, it will keep you awake at night.

 ALERT

Vivid colors of any hue will interfere with a restful night's sleep. Similarly, avoid the day-brightness of solid white; use it sparingly.

Instead of using bright or glossy white, try off-white, like eggshell or cream. Soft yellow, for instance, is considered an excellent color for a bedroom and is very conducive to a good night's rest. Gentle, warm colors, like some shades of pink, are exceptionally soothing.

Very strong colors, including deep purple, red, and orange, are too strong for a relaxing bedroom. Green and blue are cool colors, better off in the bathroom or elsewhere in the home, and probably should be saved for accent, rather than serving as the dominant color scheme. Light green is preferable to dark, and dark blue, like the color of deep bodies of water, should be avoided.

The same is true for patterns. Busy wallpaper and/or carpet will keep you buzzing all night long. Also avoid the skins of dead animals in your bedroom, including sheep or leopard skin. Solid, soft colors, fabrics, and textures, preferably of natural materials, are your allies in winning a nice, long rest.

Night Lighting

It's generally recommended that overhead lighting not be used in a bedroom because of the intensity of light that will shine over your bed. Remember, too, that light is energy and therefore must be taken into account when the switch is on.

 ESSENTIAL

Remember: It is generally best to keep computers and other electrical devices out of the bedroom if you want peaceful sleep. Electricity is forced energy, and therefore can interfere with good sleep.

Even when the lights are off, however, electrical current continues along its merry way, affecting the energy flow in your bedroom and, ultimately, your ability to sleep. Rather than an overhead light—and that includes single or dual reading lamps that some bedrooms feature—try standing lamps or table lamps off to the side, not shining directly over your bed.

Room for Romance

Not all of your time in bed is spent sleeping, of course. And if you're very fortunate, you have a wonderful, loving partner with whom to explore other possibilities. If you would like such a partner but do not presently have one, don't despair—feng shui can help you in the romance department, too. With a little planning in your furniture purchases and arrangement and your bedroom decor, you can attract the relationship you desire.

Starting Over

If you have recently ended a long-term relationship, and you can afford to do it, consider buying a new mattress. A bed, like other furnishings, absorbs the energy of the people who sleep in it, and you don't want any "old business" casting a shadow over your new relationship.

Throw away the holdover, sentimental pieces from your past relationship(s)—the theater or concert stubs and programs, old pictures, small gifts, souvenirs of trips together, et cetera. If you can't part with them altogether, at least keep them out of your relationship area.

You want to attract a new person and a new way of relating to that person. After all, if your old habits were effective, you wouldn't be looking for someone new!

 FACT

The end of a relationship is the perfect time for a clearing. Clear your space, certainly, but also consider freshening up or changing other elements of your bedroom. Your intentions will be for personal renewal, but they should also aim to change and improve the energy flow.

Art Inspires Life

In your bedroom, your artwork should depict happy, loving couples, not wistful-looking men or women sitting all alone. Nor is it a good idea to have pictures of lonely looking, wave-battered cliffs, or isolated islands or rocks surrounded by a cold, blue sea and ominous, gray skies.

You should have pairs of objects in your relationship bagua, located in the right-hand corner of the room as you are looking into the room from the doorway. For instance, a picture of a loving couple (or pair of birds), a pair of red candles, or two heart-shaped boxes. Some consultants suggest throwing sexy red lingerie into the corner and, in this particular area of the bedroom, hanging a round mirror to keep the energy moving.

Be sure to keep your relationship corner clean—no dirty laundry, cobwebs, or dust bunnies. Red is the color of passion, and so some red in your relationship corner is desirable, even though you don't want that to be the color of your whole room. Symbols of romance and togetherness, such as hearts or a pair of doves or lovebirds, are ideal in that corner, especially since these birds mate for life.

 ALERT

> Erotic art can be appropriate in the bedroom, but refrain from displaying it in public areas of your house.

Incorporating elements of feng shui works not only for attracting a new relationship, but also for enhancing one you have. Just keep your intention clear and positive, and don't place dried or wilted plants or flower arrangements in your relationship corner, since they represent death and decomposition (and you don't want these things to happen to your relationship!).

A Welcoming Space

Beyond your relationship corner, your entire bedroom should be set up for two, even if one is still your loneliest number. You should have two nightstands, one on either side of the bed, for instance, and a double or queen-sized bed, rather than a twin bed, which screams, "I'm still single!"

Make your bedroom appear welcoming to a special someone who might want to spend some time there with you. It should offer an obvious place for this person to put his or her clothing and other personal items without feeling too awkward about it. The room should, in other words, look like you were expecting company rather than building a private fortress or retreat.

Some lighter, brighter, more whimsical furnishings or decorative pieces are helpful, too, because a loving relationship includes lightheartedness and fun. Avoid having a television, computer, VCR, and DVD, as well as workspace, in your bedroom, because these will distract and detract from your relationship as well as disrupt the energy flow of your room. The only way around this in feng shui is to keep these electrical items tucked away in a small entertainment cabinet with cupboard doors that close when the item is not being used. To get the best sleep, turn all of these things off when you feel yourself nodding off to dreamland.

More on Décor

In keeping with the general advice about bedroom colors, take inventory of yours. Blues connote isolation, for instance. Warm earth colors, on the other hand, encourage closeness. In addition to having pairs of furnishings, you will want to achieve balance throughout the bedroom. Women whose rooms are ultrafeminine should consider adding some neutral or more masculine décor, and vice versa, to allow for a mix of yin and yang, which is ideal in relationships.

Balance larger, heavier furnishings with some smaller, lighter ones. Arrangement of the bed and other furniture should be conducive to good energy flow, and mirrors, except maybe for a small one in your relationship corner, should be avoided. Assess whether all areas of your room are open to the touch of another person, or are you still, in some way, holding back by guarding some precious items that you think of as being for you, alone? Ideally, the person you hope to attract into your life, and your bedroom, will eventually add some touches of his or her own, but the attitude and energy established by you before that point are critical.

 ALERT

Mirrors over the bed invite trouble into a relationship, possibly even leading to one person in it becoming involved with someone else.

Bed Position

Do not sleep with your feet facing the door. The death, or coffin, position, as it is known, is symbolically highly unlucky. If you pay attention to chakra points, you will also know that the ones in your feet will be drained as you sleep if your feet are facing the door.

You want the bed to point toward a wall in such a way that you still are in view of the doorway (preventing vulnerability), but not directly in line with it. This is also known as the emperor's position (regardless of whether you're in a king-sized bed!). Keeping all of your energy intact can only improve your love life, right?

 ESSENTIAL

> Instead of placing your bed against a wall, keep the space free on both sides of the bed for ideal energy flow. As noted elsewhere in this chapter, the space should be free under the bed, as well.

A Balanced Position

When yin and yang lack harmony, they destroy each other. If something is yin, therefore, it must face in that direction. Also, if your home is on a slope in which left and right sides are uneven, negatively affecting yin and yang, you might have some trouble dating and mating.

I'd advise seeking out a feng shui expert who may use intuition or take compass readings (using a luo pan or geomancer's compass) to determine possible disturbances in energy flow, if you suspect this is a problem.

In general, though, it's best to have your bedroom in the back of the house and to pay close attention to what you place in your relationship corner, the far right corner as you face the room from the doorway. Think red, hearts, candles, pairs of objects, pictures of happy couples, sexy lingerie, perfume, love poetry, and erotica.

That's the corner that will help you turn the corner in your love life, so treat it well—make clutter off-limits here for sure.

 QUESTION

How can using feng shui improve romance?
If you want to have more love in your life, consider buying a pair of lovebirds and positioning them in the upper right-hand corner of your bedroom. What is more mindful than putting a pair of birds that mate for life in your relationship corner?

A Sensual Experience

Mood music, aromatic candles, soft lighting, soft colors, and soft fabrics all contribute to a sexier bedroom, as well. The art of seduction lies in soothing and sensual, not loud and brassy.

It also helps to relocate the family reunion from the bedroom to another room in the house. That is, remove pictures of your mom and dad, your kids, and your siblings from your bedroom walls. Who can feel sexy and uninhibited with these eyes on them? You might as well douse yourself with cold water and throw on some flannel!

Chapter 8

Removing Energy Blocks in the Bathroom

If the front door of the house is the mouth of chi and the kitchen is the stomach, the bathroom is without doubt the internal plumbing. This plumbing ties in to your personal chi as well, and you can suffer from a clutter-filled bathroom unless you pay attention to cleanliness and order. Think about what you truly need in the bathroom (have you looked in your medicine cabinet lately?) in order for it to be the center of cleanliness it is intended to be.

The Bathroom as Metaphor

More than anything else, the bathroom is used for cleansing. Either you are cleansing the outside of your body in a bath or shower, or you are cleansing the inside of your body by expelling waste. So, it follows that your bathroom itself should be as clean as possible. Your bathroom, simply put, is a metaphor for how you care about yourself in terms of cleanliness, which is even more about how you present yourself to the outside world.

The bathroom also has associations with wealth, since a poorly designed, decorated, or maintained bathroom connotes little wealth and prosperity. Conversely, a bathroom in excellent working condition, with an aesthetically pleasing décor, shows the world that you are both health-conscious and prosperous.

Keep Only What You Need Today

Your bathroom should not be host to mold, half-used shampoo samples, a threadbare towel collection, every toothbrush you've had since eighth grade, or any other such remnant from the past. This is a place for cleansing and purging for the health and well-being of your entire family—so make it a place that respects this sacred purpose and its more practical purpose of good hygiene.

We are constantly bombarded by advertising for the latest products that will help us achieve the nirvana of "good-looking" chi. Each shampoo or toothpaste is better than the last, with improved conditioners or extra emollients that will make us appear younger and more beautiful. Every day, our mailboxes are filled with samples—and each time we go shopping, the cosmetic companies entice us with promotional packages filled with more makeup than we can ever use in one lifetime.

What can we do about an overabundance of products that might someday, in the distant future (when we have more time), improve our lives? Simply put, in the practice of feng shui, you can only concentrate on the here and now. The future is meaningless, so when you receive more than you can use, consider making a donation to others who can use the products in the present. Homeless shelters can use shampoos and toiletries all the time, so bag up all that you cannot use this very instant and drop them off at your local shelter!

 ALERT

Makeup has a more limited shelf life than you might think. Every six months or so, you should replace eye makeup in particular to avoid contamination and resulting eye irritation.

Squeaky Clean

Begin by clearing the countertop of any item you don't need, even if it looks good there. In feng shui, we ultimately want things that are visually appealing yet useful to us in some way, even if their only purpose is to balance elements or slow down rushing chi.

Color is also important to the cleanliness issue because too much color in the bathroom can make it appear full and unsanitary. The best color choices for bathrooms are white and soft, warm tones in the honey beige family. If you want to use your bathroom as more of a peaceful escape, you should lean toward the warm earth tones like yellow and brown to minimize any negative energy, or even use a faux marble finish to add an aura of softness and luxury simultaneously.

Clutter removal in the bathroom should be done in conjunction with the five senses: taste (old toothpaste, mouthwash, and dental floss); sound (minimizing echoes with soft, sound-dampening towels); touch (removing rough towels and excess exfoliating tools); smell (old perfumes, too many air fresheners or candles, mold and mildew); and sight (too many items scattered throughout the bathroom or on shelves).

 ESSENTIAL

Clean toothbrushes and hairbrushes on a weekly basis and replace them regularly to avoid unhealthy accumulations. Germs can multiply in a short period of time with these items, especially in households where there are several people living together.

Don't forget the other order of business in the bathroom: cleaning sinks, toilets, tubs, shower stalls, and floors. These clutter-magnets, with added moisture from water sources, require regular attention to curb negative chi.

Mindful Décor

Once you have a clean, pristine white bathroom interior, you should decorate with hues of blue and green, since these colors will help you relax and your drainpipes to flow freely. Color psychologists agree that the color blue can actually reduce stress levels by lowering blood pressure, while green provides rest from eyestrain and has a calming effect similar to a soft, green field.

Some feng shui consultants will tell you that red is a good bathroom color for those who have difficulty waking up in the morning, but think about this powerful color carefully. The bathroom is often the last room you are in before retiring to your bedroom at night. Red is a fire color, and while it can wake you in the morning, it can also keep you up for a restless night. Plus, the water elements in the bathroom will "put out" the fire element of red, making it less effective anyway.

In terms of décor items to include in your bathroom, choose simply and wisely. Instead of groupings of small knickknacks, which are challenging to keep clean in a frequently used bathroom, place a few relaxing paintings or pictures on the walls and choose a soft, simple window dressing. Consider building lots of storage cabinets for towels, toiletries, and supplies versus leaving all out in the open for family and guests to see. Just as in Victorian times, matters of the toilette are best kept private.

Keeping It Clean: Bathroom counters should contain only the necessities such as soap and toothbrushes. Store all other items.

All of your bath and beauty products in your bathroom closet should be limited to the ones you use on a regular basis—keep all the sometimes-used extras stored in a plastic bin in the hall closet, and remember to pitch the ones you no longer use!

Of course, you can also store the bath products you use daily on a shower rack. Choose from either the one that hangs over the showerhead or the suction-cup version. Many bed and bath shops have interesting and fun options for shower storage—it doesn't need to be boring or plain.

For medicine chests, a good storage solution is to use small plastic baskets that can neatly hold several small items. Store all like items together (e.g., medicines in one basket, hair clips in another) and put first aid items in a spot where they will be easily accessible, even in the dark.

 ESSENTIAL

If you have old plumbing in your home, be sure to have a "pipe cleaning" once a year to keep things flowing properly. Hair and waste buildup is also clutter.

All of your cleaning materials are best stored in a closed cabinet that is not accessible by children. You'll want them to be close to the bathroom when emergencies occur, and storing them in the laundry room or under the kitchen sink will not help you as quickly should a problem occur. Plastic handyman bins (with a handle in the middle) can be perfect solutions, as they are very accessible and can quickly provide you with all of the cleaners you could possibly need at a moment's notice.

Finally, if it doesn't cause you to stress out, it's okay to keep a scale in the bathroom. But if weight is a constant challenge, perhaps a better place to keep it would be in a hall closet.

Free-Flowing Energy

To keep you and your family healthy and well, energy needs to flow freely throughout your bathroom. If you've planned everything well and addressed potential clutter issues, the chi will come in through the door, drift around through the floors and then up the walls, and finally move gently through an open window. The porcelain fixtures help chi work its way through the bathroom in a smooth, waterlike fashion.

In this way, the chi mimics the water element contained in the bathroom itself, and this creates a harmonic balance.

Keeping the Energy Moving

Ceiling fans in the bathroom can get the energy flowing, making stagnant chi get a move-on. Some feng shui practitioners spray aromatherapy scents into ceiling fans before turning them on, so that the scents quickly dissipate throughout the room. You can do this for an interesting sensory effect.

When there is a significant amount of clutter, chi is inhibited and bumps into boxes, overstuffed storage shelves, dirt on the floor—and then it can ricochet off of a closed or dirty window. Clothes left on the floor also hold chi down. In this scenario, the chi becomes scattered and breaks apart, creating disharmony and the potential for illness or stress.

The ideal situation is one in which the chi can freely enter the bathroom, glide around and through it, and then continue on its merry way outside and around your home. Each time healthy chi flows through the room, we enhance our experience of the room as a peaceful escape—a place where we can re-energize and revitalize our spirits.

 ALERT

> Earth overpowers water, so using earth tones (and earthlike elements like faux marble) will keep the water from draining out—and keep your wealth in your family!

Windows, Mirrors, and Walls

What about tiles on the walls? These can be okay in terms of their reflective qualities (water), especially if you have a small bathroom that needs to be symbolically enlarged. For example, if a bathroom has pink and blue glass tiles, which can be lovely but also great stress-reducers, this bathroom can be a great place for an unwinding luxury bath any night of the week. But mirrored tiles are not a good idea in the bathroom, since these create a wealth-constricting effect that keeps the money contained rather than flowing.

However you decide to adorn your windows, mirrors, and walls, do keep them clean. Hair can accumulate on mirrors and walls, courtesy of the blow dryer, as well as on floors, courtesy of the brush. Hairspray can create a sticky buildup on windows and mirrors. Toothpaste can splash onto mirrors and walls, too.

Watch out for these kinds of "residue" clutter, and remember that while cleanliness is key to good feng shui in every room of the house, it's especially critical in the bathroom for the purpose of your family's health and well-being. Don't forget to check out the wall behind the bathroom door—it's a favorite hiding spot for dust, dirt, and hair buildup.

Check walls for peeling paint. Unless you've painted the walls with waterproof paint (a good idea in the bathroom), moisture can make walls crack and peel. Mold can also create cracks and buildup on shower walls, forcing you to recaulk several times. Prevent this time-consuming situation with a shower-cleaning spray after each use—or at least once a week.

 ESSENTIAL

> Store towels in a hall closet, keeping only a few clean ones on your towel racks. Or be creative and bring balancing earth elements into the room with a woven basket with rolled clean towels for everyone in your home. Practical and grounding!

Behind the Medicine Chest

Feng shui consultants love mirrors for their reflective and space-enhancing magic. Just keep them useful and away from one another in larger bathrooms, since dueling mirrors can block energy. Mirrors that break up the image can split the energy they give off, so it's generally best to have a nice round mirror that is one brilliant piece.

If you don't have a round mirror, you can soften the hard edges of a square one by framing it or by having the glass cut in the corners to keep chi flowing and avoid "poison arrows" (hard angles or edges that seem to "point" to you in a way that's symbolic of negative energy). Willow twigs in a clay jar next to the mirror will also help counter this problem.

 ESSENTIAL

> Be as mindful in the things you keep in your bathroom as you are in other rooms of your home, and you will never want for what you truly need.

In feng shui, bathroom mirrors work best if they are simply flush with the wall, or function solely as mirrors. So, the protruding and multifunctional medicine chest is less than ideal. It can still work in the feng shui bathroom as long as it is kept clean and clutter-free. The problem with many medicine chests is that they tend to become the storage bin for things that "might" get used someday (misplaced energy) or, worse yet, for things that are now useless (stagnant chi). Hoarding things, even small items like makeup and tweezers, can block your prosperity by keeping new things from coming into your life, and keeping expired medications can even be dangerous.

Scenes from a Stress Junkie's Bathroom

Bathrooms can suffer from the same "blocked chi" feeling as cluttered kitchens, offices, or garages. They can be a major source of turmoil, especially for the stress junkies out there. You can probably tell a stress junkie when you see one: He or she is always "on," always living on the edge of several simultaneous deadlines. Here are some other telltale signs:

Mismatched Colors and Styles

The bathroom décor is sloppy and haphazard. Nothing seems to match—or even coordinate well—in the stress addict's bathroom. Pictures, towels, and accessories aren't even close to the same color family or in the same style. A Martha Stewart nightmare!

 ESSENTIAL

> Don't just empty, but also clean the trashcan in your bathroom. Letting dirt accumulate under trash can make it a breeding ground for germs—and can signify stress in your life. When you clear clutter, clear it all!

Reading to Catch Up On

Another sign of stress is an abundance of unrelated items in the bathroom. Stress junkies try to pack so much into their days, that there is little time set aside to relax anywhere. So, they stack piles of unread mag-azines or books near the toilet or tub. This way, they reason, they can read while bathing or, well, you know.

Clutter Everywhere

The stress addict is 100 times more likely to have dirty towels piled on the back of the door or on the floor, with dirty clothes thrown in, too. On the coun-tertops, you'll find scads of near-empty toiletries and razors that should've been pitched years ago. Don't even look in the cupboards—you can only imagine . . .

Dust and Dirt Abound

Remember, the whole purpose of the bathroom is cleanliness. The stress addict more than likely has dried flowers with cobwebs in the bathroom, soap dishes so full of residue you could probably carve out another bar, or dust and stains or spots that were never wiped up.

 ALERT

Don't forget to clean the inside of the tooth-brush holder as well. Moisture in such enclosed places can be an excellent breeding ground for mold spores—and you don't want to put mold into your mouth the next time you brush!

If you are a stress addict or know one, the best thing you can do is apply feng shui to the bathroom, then create an oasis for total relaxation (as described in the following section). Not only will you notice a marked difference in the flow of positive energy in and beyond the bathroom, but you'll also notice that greater wealth abounds. Be sure to do a space-clearing ceremony after you clear all the clutter—you'll want to start the feng shui process with a clean slate!

Creating a Spa Oasis

Aside from being a place of cleanliness, your bathroom can be a sanctuary for relaxation and renewal. But how do you create a spalike atmosphere and still follow the principles of good feng shui?

Just as you did with the kitchen, you need to appeal to all senses, mixing your "personal indulgences" with the five elements in a balanced, yin-yang way that makes for a winning combination of nature and nurture.

 ESSENTIAL

Keeping the space clean and visually appealing will appeal to your sense of sight, as will good lighting and soft, curved shapes in your bathroom versus dark, angular areas.

Creating a "no stress" zone in your bathroom can be done in a weekend, but if the thought of a complete overhaul creates more stress than it would seem to relieve, do it in small bits and pieces, one piece at a time. Each time you add something new, it will feel like a new experience—one step closer to the new, totally balanced you!

Before you start to create a bathroom that offers peaceful retreat and restful relaxation, be sure to clear the clutter and clean the bathroom. You should also do a space clearing before every spa experience to maximize the health and well-being of your time alone.

Keep Things Fresh

Air the room out regularly by opening a window whenever you can, or by circulating the ceiling fan after each use of the bathroom. Fresh air is important to your health and also to the cleanliness of the bathroom. Opening the window also brings in a nice breeze while you are having your luxury bath—and simple, natural pleasures like this are truly wonderful and soothing. Airing out a clean bathroom can create an air of positivity that is sure to be appreciated by all who use your bathroom.

Make your bathroom a place of peaceful retreat and tranquility—a place where you can escape the worries of everyday life. Keep the clutter to a minimum and you will feel the difference within and around you!

Chapter 9

When Toys 'R' U— and U 'R' Tired: Decluttering with Kids

Ever feel like you're swimming against the tide—and the tide is winning? You may feel swept away at home by all the clutter your kids create: clothing and shoes, toys and books, computer games, CDs, DVDs, magazines, stuffed animals. The list seems endless. It seems that as the kids grow, the type of clutter may change, from rattles to skateboards, but the amount never lessens. The rising pile may even seem to grow along with them. Until now, anyway.

Turning the Tide

Now is when you transform this tsunami into calm waters. You can free yourself and your family from drowning in clutter, but not the way you usually do—by doing all of the work yourself, only to have your children immediately re-create their piles of junk on your freshly cleared tables and floors. No, this time the clutter can be eliminated with the assistance of your offspring, who, you will be glad to discover, are not *really* genetically programmed to create messes in your home. And you also will have the help of some useful feng shui tips, not to mention a few new storage containers. Soon, not only will you turn the tide, but you will even be riding the wave.

Trouble in Playland

Ever notice how kids' rooms in TV shows and movies or kids' picture books are always nice and neat, with plenty of shelves and everything nicely organized? The beds are always made, the floors are always cleared, and the rooms look like the kids have never really lived in them. That's because they haven't. However, your kids, in real life, are living in their rooms—the operative word being "their." You have to be careful not to let your ideas of how a room should look overshadow the fact that the room belongs to your child and should be an expression of his or her personality.

This does not preclude having a neat or well-organized room, but it does mean that it should be up to your child as to what that organization will be. This is, after all, your child's space—the place where he or she goes to spend time, reflect, study, play, and visit with friends. Of all the places in the world, this one is the most reflective of his or her personality. It is your child's sanctuary, much as your bedroom most likely is for you now and was when you were a child yourself.

 ESSENTIAL

A child's bedroom is the external reflection of who he or she is internally. To impose your order on your child's room is to send the message that your child does not have choices, even about his or her own space, and that when he or she does make choices, those choices are somehow "wrong."

Working together, you can find a solution that will please you both, bring some order to the chaos, and also give your child self-confidence in making decisions about his or her environment. If your child is allowed to take ownership of his or her bedroom, that room is much more likely to be maintained than it will be if your child is merely told how you want things to be.

Everything in Its Place

The kind of clutter that should be of real concern with regard to achieving good energy flow is not the transient clutter that shows up or is removed day to day but the items that tend to stay put, gathering dust, for weeks or months. It's good to have a plan of attack for how to organize all the little things that can build up in a child's room.

Look at Books

One mom who enlists the aid of her children in cleaning their rooms always starts with their books. Often, enough time passes between thorough cleanings that your child will have outgrown a few or several of his or her books. Kids love the idea that 1) they are a "big" boy or girl and now have outgrown a particular book, and 2) they can share this book they have enjoyed with other children by giving it away to a school, library, or charity. Allowing children to decide whether to donate their books teaches them compassion, while also clearing some space.

 ALERT

> If your child is reluctant to let that book go, even if you think he or she truly has outgrown it, don't push too hard. Just have your child put it on the bedroom or playroom bookshelf and try again another day. The decision rests with your child, and, after all, there is nothing wrong with hanging on to an old friend.

You can encourage your child by explaining that this donation makes some room for a new book or two, too. Or, you can plan more frequent visits to the library with your child, where he or she has a wide selection—and where the books eventually will return, freeing your child's space for improved energy flow.

Books are a good place to begin, too, because there are obvious, easy ways of organizing them—alphabetically by title or author, topic, size and color, and so forth.

Pick Up Those Clothes

Clothes are next. They have to be tried on, and therefore they are more time-consuming than books, but they are easily organized: They either fit or they don't; they either need cleaning or repair or they don't; and they either belong folded in a drawer or hung on hangers in the closet. Or—sometimes—they need to be folded and placed in a box for the next child in line or to be donated to charity, with clear labeling on the box as to the type and size of clothing inside.

Now Where Does *This* Go?

Next is basically everything else—toys, drawings, projects, and miscellaneous possessions. These are the things that will require the most creativity, time, and effort to organize. But when you do this with your child, acting as a team, make a game of it and think creatively, you actually can have some fun organizing. The result is more likely to be a creative arrangement that not only reflects your child's personality but also, if done right, will inspire your child to maintain it. Approach this task with a sense of adventure and fun, if your child is young, or with a stylish, creative flair, if your child is older. You should choose containers and bookcases together. Also consider a new throw rug or two; an inexpensive chair or beanbag seat; and a small, inexpensive magazine rack, end table, or nightstand to help organize while making the room look better.

 ALERT

> Avoid under-the-bed storage; this prevents the free flow of chi, which could disrupt sleep. If redecorating, also avoid installing mirrors that can be seen from the bed, because reflections also inhibit chi and, therefore, sleep. And, again, be certain that neither the foot or the head of the bed is facing the door.

Putting It All Away

Generally, it's recommended that you have more storage containers and space than items in your child's room. This certainly makes it easier to put everything away, because then you don't have to sort through all of it each day. Shelves, of course, allow kids to see what they have, while containers allow for putting away oddly sized toys or toys with lots of pieces. Play mats for small children or sheets, blankets, or tablecloths for older ones are also good because when they are done, kids can fold up the mat or blanket and put everything away.

 ESSENTIAL

> Roll-up mats can be purchased for jigsaw puzzles. The puzzles can be rolled inside the mat at the end of the day and unrolled the next when the child is ready, without disturbing the pieces that already have been put together or misplacing the loose pieces.

Naturally, boxes and baskets are good for cleanup as well as for taking toys from one room to another. Kids enjoy decorating their containers, which is an excellent way to enlist their participation in organizing their belongings. Allow them to draw on the boxes and other containers, and maybe even add stickers, glue on pictures from magazines, or make other creative and colorful additions. They will then be more likely to want to use these personalized containers.

When searching for containers, remember that the younger the child, the more likely the need for low shelves and containers that can be stacked on the floor— but not too high. If you are considering toy boxes, make sure they are safe, and that they have safety hinges that prevent the lids from slamming down on little fingers. You also want to avoid lids that latch or are so heavy they can't be lifted or opened easily by your child if he or she should climb inside the toy box. Antique toy boxes may be pretty, but they are not appropriate for your child if they do not meet these safety requirements.

Whatever storage containers you purchase or make, they, like the clutter they are designed to hold, should be put away neatly and, ideally, organized in such a way that, if they are not transparent, your child still knows what they hold. Like the boxes of hand-me-down clothing, labeling is a good idea. Keeping art supplies in one container, blocks in another, and dolls and doll accessories in yet another is a very good way to help your child keep track of his or her things. It also makes playtime less frustrating—more time for play, less time spent searching for favorite items. Also, having everything in one box makes it easier to transport that game or type of toy and its accessories to one of their friends' houses.

 FACT

Some blocks, games, and other toys come in sturdy containers that will last as long, if not longer, than the toys themselves. Some blocks also come in dual-purpose containers—the containers serve as platforms for the blocks while the child plays with them and then stores the blocks when they are through. Great idea!

Containers, it should be noted, are only useful when they are used! Encourage your child to play with only one toy or type of toy at a time, and to put that away before taking out the next toy. Set a time of at least a half hour before bedtime for your child to put away toys and other items so that they are not left out until the next morning or beyond. You can make a game of it for your child, such as setting a timer and playing "beat the clock." This works best with children who are old enough to clean up after themselves, so that you won't become too involved in the process yourself. Otherwise, you may find that your child will not get into the habit of picking up his or her things unless you are there to help each time. Or for a larger cleanup project, especially with younger children, offer to take "before" and "after" pictures, or let your child do so.

 ESSENTIAL

Be creative, but be consistent, and whenever possible, let your child take the lead. If you give your child an allowance, nightly cleanup might be part of what is expected in order for him or her to collect. But whatever your approach, be sure to praise a job well done!

More "Kid Clutter" Spots

It's a good idea to have attractive toy boxes or containers in other rooms of the house where you allow your children to play, including family rooms and sunrooms. Clutter can accumulate in all kinds of places, and that includes the bathroom. Having a mesh bag that hangs over the bathtub spigot or shower head will help keep the bath toys in one place, as well as allow them to dry in between baths.

Here's something else to consider: Often, our kids have too many things altogether, either because we buy them, or well-intentioned friends and relatives do so. If you're not willing to give away some of these toys, especially any duplicates, then consider storing them in an attic or basement and occasionally bringing them down, emptying the boxes, and refilling them with other toys and putting these aside. In this way, you will cut down on clutter and you also will keep your children interested and entertained by toys they either did not remember having or just haven't seen for a while. Toys coming down from the attic will be seen almost like presents, and it's less expensive to rotate than to add or replace. Make the switch when your child is not around, however. You may find that he or she never wants to part with any item, meaning that this is not the right time for cleanup teamwork!

Creative Use of Space

Sometimes, we get so caught up in what to put in certain room spaces and how to place those items that we overlook what may be an even better option—what not to put in those spaces! Part of the problem of too much clutter may be too many pieces of furniture. Not only can every available surface attract still more clutter, thus increasing the problem exponentially, but not having some space in which to spread out can make it difficult for kids to create their own play areas. Having space encourages more physical activity and creativity—a place to build a chair-and-blanket fort, for example, or a place to build and leave up for a few days your creations of blocks or cushions. In short, they need a place to imagine. This could be a corner of your family room, den, or basement, or in your child's bedroom. Wherever you allow it, this is a space in which less truly can be more in terms of becoming a welcome platform from which to launch all kinds of creative play.

 ESSENTIAL

Floor coverings for this area may be appropriate and, depending on their design, even enhance imaginative play. Also helpful are cushions or pillows, giving kids a soft landing spot as well as elements with which to create interesting games. And these can be stacked neatly when the kids are done for the day.

If they have a means of creating hiding places, like small forts, or are allowed the use of sleeping tents, then you even may find that clutter is contained within those places. Kids love being in enclosed places and are likely to stock them with some of their favorite books and toys. That way, these items will be where your kids can find them, yet hidden away inside their "caves" and "camps," rather than scattered about the living room for all to see—and trip over.

Don't forget about wall space, especially where your child plays. A bulletin board or two can be wrapped in colorful fabric to complement the colors in the room, and your child's latest masterpieces can be displayed there, or even their calendars of school activities and awards. Better to have a changing exhibition of creations, posters, and information than heaps of papers everywhere. In this way, not only will the room look tidier, but your child's creativity will also be nurtured.

 ALERT

Remember that you can follow the bagua while setting up your child's room and/or play space, and even while organizing the clutter— papers and books in the knowledge corner, for example; coin collections and toy banks in the prosperity corner.

Cleaning with Kids

When your children are too young to help you clean up, but old enough to make a mess, you must remain diligent about clearing the clutter and washing and cleaning their playthings—whether those are truly toys or kitchen implements with which they enjoy playing.

Even more important, perhaps, is keeping older children's clutter separate from your baby's or toddler's. Older children's toys have smaller parts than do baby toys, and these are a choking hazard for younger children. Older children often are quite helpful if trained from the time that the younger sibling begins to crawl. They will help pick up their own toys if they can be motivated, such as by the reminder that not only will their baby brother or sister stay safe, but their toys will also remain safely theirs. They should be encouraged to keep their own things in their own rooms, preferably with the doors closed to younger siblings, especially when big brother or big sister is not in the room. Older siblings should also be urged to keep their toys on shelves too high for their younger siblings to reach, or in drawers and boxes that are kept closed and would be difficult for their little brother or sister to open.

You can make a game of cleanup with the older sibling by getting down on your hands and knees with the child to crawl through each room in which they have been playing to see whether either of you discovers any small toy or piece that the younger sibling might accidentally come across. This is the same process that is recommended for checking to be sure that all electrical outlets are covered and no tablecloths hang so low that crawling babies can injure themselves.

From the time that your child can walk, bend, and pick up objects, you can begin training your child to help clean up his or her mess each day. Use a lightweight basket, laundry hamper, or large bag, and go through the various rooms in which your child has played, soliciting his or her help in gathering up items and placing them in the container. The more enjoyable you make this—conversing, singing a song together, or turning the process into a treasure hunt—the easier and quicker the process will be. You also could enlist your young child's help in cleaning up other clutter in the house, giving him or her a greater sense of belonging in the family, and wanting to make a more pleasant space for everyone. Young children love helping and feeling needed and useful.

 ALERT

> Remember that very young children not only like to put things into containers, but also like to take them out! You may want to keep your eye on that part of the process and allow a little extra time while cleaning up. Also, watch out for their wanting to "clean up" items that belong on surfaces, like knickknacks, throw pillows, or doorstops.

The main point is that everyone in the family recognizes the importance of cleanup each day, and that it can be done with your children's assistance from the time that they are very young. Also important is to recognize that cleanup can be made fun and used as another opportunity to educate, play, help, and bond with one another. Our relationships with our children don't always have to be complicated and conflicted. Like ensuring the flow of chi in our rooms, we can make life simpler and more enjoyable with our kids, creating a greater flow of chi between us all, as well.

And What Do *You* Do?

One question to ask yourself is this: What kind of example are you setting for your children with your own clutter? Often, we clean up our living rooms and dining rooms, in case we have company, if not merely for our own satisfaction. But what about our own personal spaces that guests don't usually see—our bedrooms, bathrooms, and home offices? Are there papers and books piled everywhere and closets overflowing with clothes, shoes, and odds and ends? Are there old magazines next to the bed or piled on the nightstand, along with assorted odds and ends that we never use?

 ESSENTIAL

Kids follow our lead, and if we are disorganized and allow the clutter to build up, they will feel no compunction about doing the same—and will feel justified in pointing out to us the double standard when reprimanded for their own messes.

Take advantage of the opportunity, with your younger children especially, to make it a game: "Mom (or Dad) will clean the bedroom while you clean yours. Let's see who does the best job!" Or, "Let's see who finishes first." Maybe you could pull out your old clothes, books, and objects and box them up for donation to a charity at the same time as your child is filling a box with his or her items for that purpose. Maybe you could ask your child to decorate a special container to hold your favorite items, too, or you each could decorate containers together. There is nothing like a family art project to bond parents and children, especially when the art objects will have a practical purpose and will serve as daily, visible reminders of the lovely time the two of you spent together.

Kids' Cleanup Checklist

You might find it helpful to create a checklist that both you and your kids can use in daily cleanup. Perhaps, with younger or elementary-school-aged children, you could develop a rewards system associated with this checklist—say, for every five forms filled out each week, representing at least five days of complete cleanup, they will receive five quarters, or an extra half hour of playtime before bed one evening, or some other not-too-expensive or time-consuming motivator that will ensure *consistency*. That is the key word. Without consistency, the situation could devolve to the point where clutter is overwhelming by the end of the week and seems too much for either the child or the parent to tackle.

What points should be on this checklist? That depends on your priorities in your home, but some examples might be:

❏ Put away homework papers

❏ Put away books

❏ Clear out dirty laundry and hang up/put away clean clothes, including jackets

❏ Pick up toys from the floor and other surfaces where they don't belong

❏ Throw away candy and gum wrappers and other trash

❏ Put away bath toys and hang up bath towels

❏ Clear dishes off the table and put away any food items from making snacks or school lunches

❏ Put away crayons, coloring books, markers, clay, paint, and all other similar items

❏ Put caps on and put away personal hygiene items, including toothbrushes, hairbrushes and ponytail holders, soap, shampoo, and deodorant

❏ Wipe up any messes from any of the above so that there are no sticky surfaces

It's probably a good idea to keep this checklist fairly brief so that the items can be completed and checked off in a reasonable amount of time each day. Too long a list will discourage anyone, especially a small child, and as long as the list has the basics that will keep the living space reasonably clear on a daily basis, that should suffice. Any other items can be saved for the weekend or as a special incentive to earn a little extra allowance or an additional privilege or two for the week.

Having a checklist not only will help everyone keep your home free of clutter, but it also provides some structure and expectations of responsibility that are important for growing children. And if you have your own quick cleanup checklist, as well, you will stay in step with your kids and make them feel that rather than a double standard, these are good rules for everyone to live by. Perhaps such a list will put your child on a life-long path to a more orderly household—and isn't that what your ultimate goal should be?

Chapter 10

The Great Outdoors

Ah . . . spring! Birds are singing, flowers are blooming, and finally you can open your garage door to the rest of the world. But instead of the sweet smell of roses, you catch a foul whiff of a season's worth of funk. After a long winter, you are sure to find a number of good reasons why spring is the season of the year that is famous for cleaning. It's time to clear the air with good feng shui!

Winter's Leftovers

As soon as the ice of winter begins to melt and the first buds of spring appear, it's easy to want to spend more of your time outside. Even if you're busy doing a spring cleaning inside your home, the ultimate goal is to work your way back again into the great outdoors for some peace, fun, and relaxation.

But before you can relax and enjoy the pleasures of a well-manicured yard, you must remove the remnants of winter: broken limbs, dead trees and shrubs, beds of leaves, and the first sure signs of seasonal change—weeds. Dead foliage should especially be removed as soon as possible, since anything dead can create negative chi in your surroundings. Despite the fact that spring is a time of rejuvenation and rebirth, allowing dead foliage to compost all over your yard is not a positive move in feng shui terms. Instead, you should designate one area toward the back edge of your yard as "Compost Central," and allow the "reincarnation" process to occur in a less-cluttered, more mindful manner.

Do your best to start early in the spring with a definitive plan of attack. List every detail of your yard, garden, and even garage or shed spring cleanup plan, and get busy as soon as the weather changes. Simply put—don't let the weeds win!

The Root of the Problem

We already know that inside clutter can be the result of an inability to deal with the past. The meaning of outside clutter is exactly the same; in many cases, for good or ill, the yard or the garage is the final resting place of all the things we cannot yet part with.

There are several reasons behind clutter buildup. First, as a society, we suffer from excess: We have way too much, and have access to way too much more. One trip to a Home Depot or Lowe's superstore will answer the question of why some people have so many lawn ornaments, overdone trellises, and rock gardens littering their yards. Done simply and well, these same adornments can beautify a yard—but unfortunately, some people don't seem to know where to stop with their purchases. Perhaps they have a poverty consciousness—that is, they may be so afraid of being poor that they clutter their yards with an excess of everything from dressed-up plastic geese to colorful flags and park benches.

But another underlying cause of "junk-in-the-yard" syndrome may be a feeling of being overwhelmed by life in general. Often, when our lives feel completely out of control—with too much happening and not enough time or money to deal with matters of clutter—we tend to let things go in hopes that somehow, someday, they'll take care of themselves. If this sounds like you, you might do well to practice meditation or yoga, so that you can gain the clarity you need to make better decisions. Hang in there—you can win the upper hand in the battle against clutter!

Healing the Land

Aside from removing physical clutter from the land around your home, you can also remove the clutter of years of trauma. Your land has a history that belongs to it from the beginning of time. But time can take its toll on all living things, including the ground beneath your feet.

Listening to the Land's Story

You can become one with your property by walking all around it, and then being still and listening to its story. For instance, did Indians once roam the land? One family asked for a land healing ceremony after it was discovered that a small tribe of Indians was murdered on a path that went straight through their property. Every family that had lived in the home since the time it was built on the property experienced trauma in the form of death, divorce, and financial disaster, and this family didn't want to be next. By hiring a professional feng shui consultant who was also experienced in land healings, they were able to bring peace to the land after centuries of residual trauma—and this helped to clear the land of its own emotional clutter. The family has since experienced improvements in many areas of life as a result.

Healing It Yourself

How can you do a land healing yourself? You begin by recognizing that your property may have been the site of many negative and unsettling events (including shifts in sediment). Then proceed to walk around the yard, blessing it and offering peace with flower essences (like magnolia or lavender) or crystals (such as quartz and granite) strategically placed along the meridians (dividing lines) of your yard. Flower essences and healing crystals are said by feng shui practitioners to raise the vibrational energy level of the land.

After you place these along the meridians, walk them and clear the negative chi by clapping your hands or ringing a bell. It needn't be a grandiose show for your neighbors' amusement—this is subtle and serious work, and it is an important element in good feng shui practices for the land all around you. If you're out in a public place and intuitively sense that land has experienced trauma or a disturbance of some kind, you may also conduct an on-the-spot emotional clutter removal for the land as a way of improving your experience or the enjoyment of others.

 ALERT

You can locate "Land Healers" through feng shui consultants, metaphysical bookstores, advertisements, or even the Internet, but be sure to check out any credentials or references.

Back to the Feng Shui Garden

Whether your garden is a plethora of green and reflective water, as in Monet's *Waterlilies*; a meditation garden with an altar; or an outdoor oasis filled with colorful flora and fauna, know that your garden can and will support you in all of your life's endeavors. Aside from being aesthetically pleasing, gardens are essential to your well-being. Here, you are literally planting your seeds of the future!

In feng shui, a healthy garden means, quite simply, a healthy life. Untidy gardens with rampant flowers and weeds or foliage can drain the healthy chi that surrounds your house, not to mention your own personal chi on the day when you finally do find the time to tend the garden!

One of the nice things about visiting China is seeing the beautiful simplicity of its gardens. For the Chinese, less is always more. Chinese gardens accent simplicity and usually include one tree or bush, or focus on one type of flower at a time. There are not layers and layers full of impeccably landscaped floral arrangements!

Here are some tips to keep your garden crisp and clean—the feng shui way:

1. *Alternate a succession of budding trees or flowers in bloom throughout your landscape.* Plant evergreens in each corner of your garden's bagua to ground your success and cultivate your life's potential.
2. *Contain the chi in your garden by creating boundaries or borders with bushes and shrubbery.* A fence would work, too. Creating boundaries helps keep the chi contained in your immediate surroundings, not dissipating into thin air.
3. *Create a compost area in a place that feels right*

to you. Most people drop compost over the ledge of their backyard if there's a drop-off, but you can also incorporate a composting center, so to speak, in your wealth corner. Think about it: You are taking what has grown from the earth and provided for you, and returning it to the earth for another growth cycle. This is nature's prosperity center!

4. *Invite a sense of mystery and intrigue into your garden to keep it interesting.* Add or change elements often, especially things like outdoor art or sculpture. Incorporate colorful objects of different shapes to maximize a sense of interest, wonder, and excitement in your garden.

5. *Finally, treat your yard with love and respect.* Your landscape is a living thing that "talks" to you, your family, and just about everyone else who stops by for a visit.

 ESSENTIAL

> Remember to clear garden clutter regularly—prune, weed, clear, rake, and water on a weekly basis. Overgrown gardens contain oppressive energy.

Your garden and its surroundings communicate a message to others and create a particular feeling in others, too. How many times do you hear, "Wow, is it nice and peaceful here!" That's what others should be saying to you about your garden.

Space for You to Grow, Too: When creating your clutter-free garden, don't forget to create space for yourself. You want to be able to enjoy all that healthy, flowing chi in your yard!

Building On a Good Idea: Storage Tips

Gardens can be self-contained spaces offering a plethora of organic pleasures, but they can also be home to small structures like greenhouses, sheds, or cottages.

Greenhouses come naturally equipped with their own light, so that's not an issue. But size and location are definitely important. A greenhouse should be in proportion to the landscape; it should never be so large as to overwhelm it, nor too small to perform its intended duty. Of course, a greenhouse should always be located near a water source.

 ESSENTIAL

Make your garden a peaceful, meditative retreat. Put in a small pond with a park bench next to it, or a gazebo with built-in seats. Garden stones and lighting balance out the elements, making your retreat a perfect yin-yang spot.

Sheds are perfect places to store outdoor furniture in the wintertime, or lawn accessories and tools in the summer. Just keep your shed in a good location several feet from your house—if it's too close, you'll worry about the yard work you haven't gotten to yet, but if it's too far away, well . . . out of sight, out of mind.

A small cottage or studio in your yard can be a wonderful escape from the rest of the world: a place for reading, journaling, meditating, or just plain relaxing. As with the shed, find a good location that's not too close by (you'll feel guilty when you're not able to relax) or too far away (it will always seem like you are struggling to break free from your regular routine). I used a studio at my previous home as a home office, and it was the perfect way to keep work and home life separate.

The choice of which kind of structure to include in your backyard is entirely yours, just be sure to position any poison arrows (sharp edges of the structure) away from your house so that you don't send any negative chi back toward your home. That would defeat the purpose of a peacefully intended freestanding structure.

 ESSENTIAL

Kids can have an outdoor structure like a tree house or a playhouse, which will raise the levels of the fun "fire" element in your yard. Just be sure to keep the toys from piling up— and keep them clean!

Sweeping Out the Garage

Keep your garage clean and well swept in order to maximize the flow of chi in this extra addition to your home. Don't try to make it an extension of your basement or attic—this is a place of storage for useful items such as tools and seasonal furniture, not a dumping ground for everything from ratty old toys and broken furniture to tires, file cabinets, and obsolete computer equipment.

We all know someone who keeps so much old, useless junk in their garage that they can't even think of parking their car inside. The hard truth of the matter is, you can probably get rid of more than half of what's currently in your garage and still manage to live a full, happy, and well-adjusted life.

Your garage can be a place for repairing things—for giving new life to old items. Don't let it become a morgue for all of your experiments that didn't work. Remember, in feng shui practice, it's not how much you have, but how well you keep it that counts.

So what about those useful items that you intend to keep now, and use from time to time? Storage bins can help organize these helpful items you consciously choose to store in your garage. Buy the plastic bins with the lids to minimize any chance of mildew, and be sure to label each bin with its general contents to make it easy to locate necessary items when you need them.

 ALERT

> Broken items represent death and negative, oppressive energy. All broken items that are beyond repair should be thrown away to avoid negative chi. If an item can be repaired but you no longer want it, donate it to charity or sell it at a garage sale.

The "Good Chi Garage Sale"

Having a garage sale is a great (and auspicious) way to begin your journey into the world of feng shui decluttering. By selling off excess clutter of your own and your family, you not only free up your living space, you also fill it with good chi and a few extra dollars.

If you decide to hold a "Good Chi Garage Sale," be sure to price everything to go. Assign rock-bottom prices so that you are sure to get rid of most of your stuff in one day. Then use the power of feng shui to position your soon-to-be-former belongings to sell, sell, sell!

Group like items together, and then place them on tables that are slanted a little in order to activate the flow of energy around them. We want these items to radiate their energy to bargain hunters—not get lost in a huge pile of stagnant energy that is blocked by tables crammed together!

Bring Out the Bagua

You will greatly increase the profitability of your Good Chi Garage Sale if you follow the bagua octagon in the placement of the goodies you're offering for sale. Place your most valuable items for sale on a table in your wealth corner—right near your checkout table.

 ESSENTIAL

Once a year, have a "feng shui clearing" garage sale. Get rid of any items you no longer use, like books, kitchen gadgets, CDs, and videos. Donate whatever doesn't sell to charity.

Place old photo frames in your family corner (on the far left or east side of the bagua, beneath the wealth corner) to attract shoppers who might want these photo frames to house pictures of their loved ones. For added impact, slip in a picture of a family from a magazine.

Books, videos, and old bookshelves should be placed on a table or shelf in the knowledge corner of your "Good Chi" bagua, just below the family section. Line the middle entrance of your driveway with old office furniture, equipment, or accessories, since this is the career corner. It also has the corresponding elements of water and ancestral energy, so things that pertain to those elements can also be included in this area of the garage sale. Along with the career-oriented office stuff, you might also toss in some pool toys (or an old pool itself!), as well as that ugly old lamp that your dear departed relative left you. While it may not go well with your décor, believe me when I say it will find a home somewhere else.

To the right of your "career" entrance is the helpful people corner of your Good Chi Garage Sale bagua. The elements that correspond to this corner are the heavens and travel, so here is where you might display old suitcases, photos, or posters of faraway places. You might also include any religious objects such as statues or icons.

The children's department of your garage sale should be located in the west corner of this bagua, just up from the helpful people corner. This is where you will offer all the toys your kids no longer play with and the clothes they no longer wear. In most garage sales, these are the items that get sold and resold the most! Since the corresponding element to this area of the bagua is metal, you can also include metal items such as bicycles, candlesticks, and kitchen gadgets.

Old wedding gifts you didn't use would be a good fit in the marriage corner. This area of the bagua is in the top right, between the children's area and the fame corner. You can also put pottery and earth-related items in this section, since the corresponding element is earth. Pictures of landscapes can be placed on the ground, leaning on the tables that hold the pottery and other earth-related items. If you are going through a divorce or just coming out of a failed relationship, this would also be a good place to get rid of old gifts and reminders!

The fame corner, which will be dead center in the south corner of your bagua, is the ideal place to sell anything that elevates the attractiveness of the individual (with the potential to bring fame and fortune). Remember those designer jeans you bought just in case you'd lose ten pounds? Hang 'em up here with an enticing price tag. How about the exercise equipment you bought from those famous thin people on TV? Dust it off and move it to this corner for your garage sale. And don't forget that the element that corresponds to fame is fire—making this an ideal corner to feature candles, mirrors, and fireplace tools.

Useful to the End

All of these tips may make you tired at the thought of having a garage sale. You might think you're going to a lot of extra trouble to attractively position stuff you are looking to dump anyway. But keep in mind that your possessions can serve you even as they depart your company. In other words, let your things bring you good fortune in the form of positive money energy while they are leaving your home to offer new life to another's home.

Accept the fact that you were not even using many of these items in the first place. Remember that the goal is to give up the things that no longer bring you happiness or represent who you are now, at this moment. Take a deep breath; then let go of this old, stagnant energy!

Of course, not everything will sell at your Good Chi Garage Sale. Whatever doesn't sell you must remain committed to clearing, so remember to put those items in a small pile and call the Goodwill truck immediately after your sale is over. There should be nothing—seriously, nothing—left once you're finished with a feng shui clearing like this one.

Clearing the Air

Now that you've rid yourself of all that you do not need, you can concentrate your energy on improving what's left. Perhaps it's time to paint the garage, or add a nice window in it that allows the chi to flow in a more positive direction. Or maybe, now that you've sold off the things that don't hold any meaning for you, you finally have the money (and the space) to purchase other, more useful items that will help improve your quality of life on the outside of your house.

Whatever you decide to do, you can congratulate yourself on a job well done—and one that all of your neighbors will happily notice. Sit back in your lawn chair, bask in the sunlight, and breathe in all that positive chi!

Chapter 11
Out and About

We are like snails, carrying our homes on our backs—with our backpacks, purses, wallets, briefcases, and diaper bags all stuffed full of items. We prize every coupon, coin, breath-freshener, hand mirror, pen, and package of gum. We not only lug along our home, but our offices, beauty salons, and day-care centers. Then, we complain that we can't find anything. What to do? That depends on your priorities—what you're willing to give up and how organized you are willing to be.

My Wallet, Myself

It is truly amazing what a man can fit into his wallet. Granted, a wallet may not be as jam-packed as most women's purses, but it carries its share of unused items and space-wasters. Expired coupons and a myriad of credit cards, multiple photos and old business cards, phone numbers without names and names without numbers, and ancient matchbooks.

You should start your wallet decluttering by asking yourself a simple question: "What do I really need?" That question should prompt you to discard the expired "stuff" and the nameless phone numbers and cryptic notes meant to remind you of something or someone long since forgotten. Out go the photos of you from the '80s when you still had your hair, and the ones of your kids in diapers before they had theirs. Out go the matchbooks, since you don't even smoke, and old business cards. What stays? Only the credit and business cards that are current and that you actually use on a regular basis, a current photo or two, and your current driver's license and club memberships.

 ALERT

> In this age of identity theft, the less personal information you carry, the better. Keep all of your important information, and especially passwords and Social Security cards, in a safe place at home.

You might want to treat yourself to a new, clean wallet while you're at it. Many men seem to carry theirs until they are so worn, the denomination of the paper money can be detected from the outside. A new, organized wallet is a simple and easy way to give you a lift. When you pull it out of your pocket—very easily, since it's no longer stuffed to bursting—people will see that you take good care of yourself and your belongings. They'll also notice when you can swiftly pull out what you need, without first fumbling through seven or eight out-of-date credit or business cards.

Purses: Everything but the Kitchen Sink

Women and their purses. Say the two words together, "women" and "purses," and many people immediately have an image in mind—large purse, lots of junk, confused woman rooting through it, insisting, "I know it's in here somewhere!" A picture of her husband or boyfriend first making fun of her, and then asking her to carry something in her purse for him, like his sunglasses or concert program, or requesting one of the many helpful tools or health aids she might have in there. "Honey, do you have any aspirin?" "Honey, do you have a nail file I can borrow for a moment?"—or, more often, "Honey, do you have some tissues?" Who knows? Maybe somewhere out there is a man saying, "Honey, do you have some hedge clippers?" and she is able to produce them.

You can double or triple these requests by children, for whom Mommy is a veritable packhorse. Many is the time a mother will reach into her bag and pull out a child's toy, half-eaten lollipop, cloth diaper, stuffed animal, Barbie head, juice bottle, or some mystery item that she's been toting around since her child, now happily attending medical school, was a toddler. Women worry about leaving behind something that may be of importance to their loved ones or themselves, even if it is only used once or twice a year—or once a decade. But finding it? That is another matter.

An Anchor Weighing You Down

The problem with this habit, aside from the fact that it wastes a lot of time when the owner of the purse has to search for something amidst all of that clutter, is that a very heavy purse—often on a fashionably thin strap—is a prescription for shoulder, neck, and back pain. It is not unusual for a woman to seek out a doctor's care for such a problem, only to be asked what kind of purse she carries and how heavy it is. Think of how many women haul those heavy purses around while balancing themselves on flimsy high heels. Now, there's a prescription for a lifetime of back pain! "Let's see . . . where did I put that bottle of aspirin? It's in here somewhere . . . "

Women may tell themselves that they don't have time to clean their purses, but look at all the time they spend trying to find items in those same purses. Wouldn't it be quicker and easier just to take the few minutes, or even a bit longer, to eliminate the problem? If nothing else, a true purse-cleaning is a trip down memory lane. "Oh, yes," she says as she finds a movie ticket stub, "I remember that film! And I remember Bob . . . I had to pay for the popcorn, and then he proceeded to eat the whole bucket!" Well, maybe not all of the memories are good, but the purse cleaner quickly will discover all kinds of things that she forgot she had or people she used to know, just through this simple act.

 ESSENTIAL

> While cleaning out a purse, you may ask your-self, "Just by looking at the contents of my purse, what could a future archaeologist learn about its owner?" The point to be made here is that if you have not cleaned your purse lately, you literally have been dragging the burden of your past around with you.

Purse Solutions

In order to experience the new, the different, and, we hope, the better, you need to get rid of the old—especially if that includes partially melted candy covered in lint; chewing gum that hasn't been soft since the Kennedy Administration; phone numbers of people you can't even remember meeting; and so on. And, as you will notice, all of that clutter also makes the inside of your purse dirty. Think of where your fingers go every time you reach into the depths of that mess to retrieve an item. Yuck! Say . . . do you happen to have a nail file?

A suggestion for minimizing purse clutter: Try a smaller purse (it holds less and it's not as heavy to carry) and/or an organizer purse. These are great! They have places for your cards, your pens, your cell phone, your money, and your makeup—nearly anything you can think of carrying. A place for everything and everything in its place. What could be better? You can always find what you need when you need it. This, of course, takes the intrigue out of purse carrying, but it does give you more time to spend with your family.

It's All in the Bag

Welcome to the world of daily luggage. These dependables—briefcases, backpacks, and diaper bags—are open invitations to clutter collection. Roomy and—in the case of the backpack, stuffable to nearly twice its normal size—you can get away with months, if not years, of accumulation.

Briefcases and Backpacks

What might a look into these two essentials uncover? How about old papers; business cards; presentation notes; unread books; filled notebooks; dried-up pens; broken pencils; leadless mechanical pencils; old restaurant, hotel, parking, and gas receipts; food and candy wrappers; items of clothing; old magazines; partly filled water, juice, or soda bottles; old note cards and class schedules; and handouts from various seminars and conferences, mostly unread.

Work Center to Go: Organize your briefcase with essential items in easy-to-reach locations. Loading it with stacks of papers and other items will inhibit easy access to the items you really need.

What should be in a briefcase or backpack? Only those things that pertain to your current, daily life: this year's calendar, notebooks with clean pages, usable pens and pencils, reading material for traveling or for current class work, and current phone numbers and business cards. It's helpful to have small containers or resealable bags for small items and rubber bands or paper clips to keep together paperwork. Letter-sized envelopes are good for stashing receipts; and larger, clasped envelopes are good for reports, memos, and other paperwork.

A Discreet Word about Diaper Bags

Diaper bags are a wonderful invention. One wonders what our mothers and grandmothers did without the new, ever-expanding bags made of space-age material and accommodating a seemingly endless supply of diapers, ointments, bottles, formula mixes, stuffed animals, changes of clothes, teething rings, teething biscuits, changing pads, age-appropriate toys—and even some items that actually belong to Mom and Dad but won't fit in their overstuffed purses and wallets. Packing a diaper bag is easy enough, but remembering to clean it out? Well, eventually, your nose will know.

Fermenting formula at the bottom of the bag with half-chewed teething biscuits melted in will create an interesting odor and a real mess, soiling the clean clothing and cloth diapers, stuffed animals—you get the idea. And, like our purses and wallets, paperwork will be forgotten inside—like the information on vaccinations you shoved in there at the last doctor's appointment, or the daycare paperwork that came home with your child.

A diaper bag is a clutter magnet, so it's important that you check, clean out—and air out!—the diaper bag at least once a week. It will save you time and trouble later, or even the expense of buying a new bag because the old one has become so nasty.

Living Life out of a Suitcase

Many men have no problem with this item of luggage, priding themselves on how little they can get away with.

One man traveling from Australia to the United States bragged that all he would need is a toothbrush, a few shirts, and a pair of pants, and off he would go halfway around the world. Meanwhile, his female companion confessed that she couldn't even travel around the block without packing at least two to three suitcases, just so that she could change her mind about her apparel on any particular day and would have all the shoes, belts, jewelry, and other accessories she might possibly need. Not to mention the hair dryer, makeup, shampoo, conditioner, hairspray, perfume, various skin and cleansing lotions and potions, changes of lingerie, books, magazines, address book, and so on. Oh, and the half-empty suitcase for souvenirs to pack on the return trip!

For women, sometimes it's easier just to stay home and read about traveling. But the good side of this male/female dichotomy is that as long as the man travels light, he is better able to haul the woman's bags!

Make a List, Check It Twice

Not all women travel this way, and not all men are as selective about what or how they pack. But everyone can pack smarter and cut back on clutter if they have a plan. One of the better ways to plan, and one that many people employ but then override, is to write down attire for each day of the trip, trying to make several pieces do double-duty. For instance, take only a few pairs of comfortable pants in neutral colors that can be dressed up or dressed down, and just a few accessories and pairs of shoes that can go with multiple outfits.

Wrinkle-resistant, quick-drying clothing is recommended. You don't want to have to iron—and tote one around— if you can help it.

 ESSENTIAL

> Make sure that you have a pair of dress shoes and a pair of comfortable shoes—possibly two of the latter if you will be doing a fair amount of walking. You should be able to wear one pair and pack the other.

Another good thing about a list is that it also will help you on various legs of your trip to keep track of what you brought and what needs to go home with you. Don't forget to check each item off the list as you pack.

Saving Space

There are some excellent catalogs and stores that specialize in travel goods and attire; most of these have interesting and appealing products to help you cut back on clutter. Be careful not to buy more items than you absolutely need, though. For instance, only buy the collapsible sun hat if you're sure you'll wear it often.

Most of the time, you can get by with your usual articles of clothing and accessories if you pack lightly and are smart about space conservation in your bags— folding or rolling clothes so that they are compact, nesting shoes heel-to-toe, rolling up belts and socks so they fit within the shoes, and so forth. Strategic packing will conserve space, allowing you to take enough to meet your needs and keep everything looking reasonably neat throughout the journey. Improper folding or jamming items into a bag causes wear and tear on your clothing and also consumes inordinate amounts of space.

 ALERT

Experts recommend packing your suitcase about a week before departure, allowing time to think of additional items you really need, but not so much time that you forget what you packed and throw in duplicate items, just in case. Another good reason to pack ahead is so that you can let the packed bag sit for a few days to allow contents to settle.

Be Prepared

Before going away, reopen your travel bag and look for any gaps that may have developed to put in additional items, or to remove anything you have decided you probably won't really need or use. You may find you can leave some items behind. For instance, many hotels provide hair dryers and shampoo, and so you might be able to save space by not hauling these with you.

Checking ahead on what the weather is likely to be helps; this is especially easy with the Internet weather sites. That way, you'll know if you'll really need an umbrella or a heavier jacket. A lightweight jacket or sweater, though, is always a good idea, what with the unpredictability of the weather. Will there be laundry facilities? Then perhaps you can pack fewer clothes. And if you're planning on buying a souvenir T-shirt or other clothing items, then you certainly won't need to pack as much initially. Just be sure to save room for these new items, or any other incidentals you may pick up. The one item to pack more of than you think you'll need? Underwear.

 ALERT

> If you are flying, it's especially important to pack smart and pack light. Airlines allow very few bags, and if your luggage exceeds the limit or is overweight, you will pay additional fees.

Organizing Your Bags

Keep in mind that if you are traveling alone, you will have to carry everything yourself, so being conservative is a good idea. It's also a good idea, no matter where you are flying, to have the basic necessities in your carry-on luggage in case you and your main suitcases are separated for a day or two. When baggage goes to another airport, it may take awhile before it is reunited with you, and you don't want to be caught without a change of underwear, at the very least, toiletries, and any medications you take on a daily basis. Important papers also should stay with you.

Organizing your bag is a good way of avoiding clutter. It's a good idea to pack items according to types, such as putting cosmetics and toiletries together, day clothes together, and nightclothes and lingerie together. Anything that can leak or spill, such as shampoo, perfume, or loose powder, should go in resealable plastic bags, with the air pushed out so that the bags will take up as little space as possible. Shoes should go on the bottom, with space filled in by socks, underwear, rolled-up belts, and other items. Flat items, like shirts, should be layered atop the bulkier ones. Fragile items should be cushioned in between sweaters or coats for protection.

Car Clutter

If you're not lucky enough to be flying to your destination, you will have to face your fears about cleaning up the clutter in your car and preventing the next onslaught brought about by the infamous car trip.

Many of us have childhood memories of summer road trips in which we were shoved into back seats teeming with "stuff"—suitcases, ice chests, sporting paraphernalia, shopping bags of snacks, beach bags, and our own possessions, such as pillows, stuffed animals, magnetic games, and more. Whether we are traveling alone, as a couple, or in a group, the road trip should be more about freedom and having fun than about being bogged down by a lot of luggage, which has to be hauled from car to hotel room and back out again.

ESSENTIAL

> Creating, hauling, and clearing car clutter is among the least pleasant aspects of traveling, but you can make the trip more enjoyable by clearing your car of clutter before you pack it, and by keeping your packing organized and efficient, taking only what you need and will use.

Make Room for Passengers

Even if you are not going on a vacation, you should clear the junk out of your car to make room for yourself, your guests, your groceries, and anything else you might need or want. Unnecessary junk or true trash in a car is depressing, weighing you down, and inhibiting chi, just like clutter in your home. How many of us spend at least the first few minutes of conversation with a friend preparing to ride in our car by apologizing for its appearance, before quickly scooping off clutter from the front seat and floor and sailing it over the headrest into the back? What a waste of time, not to mention the hit your self-confidence takes as you hope that the clutter will not make a poor impression on your friend—who, it is fair to say, may have an equally cluttered vehicle! And the larger the car—such as the ubiquitous minivan—usually, the greater the clutter.

It makes sense to enlist the help of your family members, if they are old enough, in cleaning the junk from the car, since you probably didn't make that pile all by yourself. As with cleaning rooms in your home, you can have more fun when there are children involved by turning this into a game—perhaps assigning different portions of the car and seeing who wins the race to clean his or her portion first, or giving a "prize" for the worst or oldest or most unusual item found, or for having the hardest portion to clean.

All that should be left are the essentials. In the glove compartment, this means your car manual, insurance card, and any maps that are pertinent to the specific place you are traveling. Suffice it to say, you no longer need that 1992 map of Florida, especially if you are not planning on going back there any time soon. Even if you did, wouldn't you want a new one? A flashlight and a tire gauge also are fine in the glove compartment, but try not to overfill it so that you don't even know what's in there and have to fight to open and close it each time.

 ALERT

Regularly clean out the drink holders, coin containers, and ashtrays and any other built-in trays designed to make your life easier by holding more "stuff." When dirty or overfilled, these can constrict the flow of positive chi for yourself and your passengers.

Trunks and Boxes

Your car trunk probably also has an overflow, perhaps because it's where you tend to throw your clutter until you "have time" to get to it. Throw out the obvious trash and then remove the seasonal items, like beach toys, when it's out of season, say, December. You should have an emergency road kit—including flares, a spare tire, a tire jack, and any tools to change the tire—a blanket or two and some bottled water either for an overheated radiator or a thirsty child. A first-aid kit is a good idea, as well.

It's not a bad idea to have a small carton in the far back or trunk in case you find or buy something that might spill or be damaged by a fall, such as a plant or a delicious but messy pie that someone gave you, or some beautiful produce you decide to buy on a whim when passing a roadside stand. Kids find lots of things, too, on outings, and many of these, such as shells or rocks, would be better off inside a box or other container. It's also helpful to keep tools and car accessories in a separate storage box with a good lid. Maps and guidebooks, which, as noted, should be restricted to those you need on a particular trip or are likely to use daily, can be kept in the door pockets.

Take Just What You Need

It's a good bet that much of what you have in your car right now is either outright trash—or maybe there are useful items that are simply not being used at present or even likely to be used in the immediate future. Maybe you have twice as many CDs or tapes as you need handy, or several pairs of shoes. You can store your music and books in padded cases made for the purpose, which keeps them together and protected. Empty your car's trash container and then use it throughout your trip rather than throwing wrappings and other trash on the seat next to you or on the floor.

Imminent car trip or no, you can't go wrong by clearing out what no longer serves you. Soon afterward, you're bound to feel like going "On the Road Again."

Chapter 12

A Home Office That Means Business

We know that feng shui is a practice—the practice of living in harmony with the energies of the earth. We also know that an important part of feng shui is balance—especially the balance of yin (the feminine, dark, cool energy) with yang (the masculine, light, hot energy). Just as we are learning to apply feng shui principles to the rest of our surroundings, it's also important to apply them to our home-based workspace.

Businesses Need Good Chi, Too

Every popular business magazine features articles detailing the importance of keeping workspaces organized and clutter-free as a key element in business success. Although clutter clearing is not in and of itself part of traditional feng shui, it is a discipline that is useful in creating "good chi" (energy) in your work-related surroundings.

There are many ways to optimize your work area. Whether you are self-employed or not, your work setting is important. But if you're an entrepreneur and your business is home-based, it is even more important to create positive, free-flowing energy. The environment you create in the workspace will emanate to the other rooms of your home, so you want to be sure you're creating an effective, "positive chi" work area.

Our talents and skills cannot be properly utilized to create wealth, success, and prosperity unless we create an atmosphere that allows them to blossom. Have you ever noticed that a messy office can leave you feeling anxious, overwhelmed, and indecisive? To be successful, your home office should instead inspire feelings of inspiration, energy, peace, and efficiency. Your office's flow of chi must be strong and full of yang to encourage a positive atmosphere.

Even if unseen, the *contents* of your filing cabinets, bookshelves, and computer files can affect your effectiveness. Overstuffed file drawers can be oppressive; old catalogs or books on the shelves tie your business to the past (instead of the future); and ancient computer files may keep you from progressing to new projects.

What should you do? First, step back from your business, metaphorically speaking, and do an assessment. How does your business "feel" to you? Does it have strong, positive vibes, or does it give off a dragging, low-energy mood? Are you getting plenty of interesting work to do, or do you feel it takes a lot of effort to obtain even the minimal number of projects you desire? Can you work effectively in your office, or do you feel your energy ebbing away as soon as you walk through the door?

 ESSENTIAL

> If your desk is cluttered with junk and the floor around you is covered with boxes, newspapers, and yesterday's lunch, your decision-making skills will be clogged. Stagnant energy will surround you; you will feel sluggish, unable to focus. This is why clutter clearing must be addressed first, before making any enhancements to your home office.

Conducting a Clutter Audit

Just reading the words "clutter audit" may make you groan. Let's face it: Few of us enjoy examining the chaos we've created by allowing clutter to build up. But, rather than avoiding this first step, embrace it. It may seem at first to be a thankless task, but analyzing your clutter is essential to creating a functional, balanced work area. It will also immediately release energy that has been stifled by the bad chi that clutter represents. More significantly, decluttering is essential to your business success. Isn't that motivation enough to get you started?

Two Critical Questions

In conducting a clutter audit, you will go through every file drawer, stack, and shelf in the office, asking yourself two critical questions: Why is this item in my office? Do I need it? If the answer is "no," immediately toss the item into a recycling or trash container. Poof! It's gone. If you do need to retain it, ask yourself: Is the place where I found it the most appropriate "home" for it? For example, is it taking up space in a key area that you need for more important items? Is it too far away from your desk? Consider its function and how often you use it. If you know you must keep the item or file in question but you get bogged down on where to keep it, just put it aside for the moment. Concentrate on the next item.

Don't get discouraged. Since decluttering can be a daunting task, you may want to divide the room into quadrants. Focus on one section at a time; try not to even glance at the other areas of the room at first. Hard to stay with it? Play some upbeat music to keep yourself moving. Give yourself a series of rewards for staying on task. For example, you could set a timer for one hour, and at the end of that time, reward yourself with a ten-minute break outside in the sunshine. Other incentives might be a couple bite-size pieces of chocolate, or playing your favorite CD. The reward can be anything that you enjoy.

Break the work down into "do-able" chunks—and don't forget to continue on with the decluttering after savoring each reward. The trick is to *make a decision*.

 ALERT

A good rule of thumb: If you haven't touched those dusty old files for at least a year, most (or all) of their contents can be archived . . . or thrown in the trash. Don't allow yourself to become paralyzed with indecision—act! You will see an increase in the energy flow around and through your office almost immediately.

Reorganizing Your System

Once you're completely finished going through all the nooks and crannies, it's time to figure out what to do with all the items you've determined you need to keep. The first step should be to decide which items should be kept near (or on) your desk, bookcase, or credenza. These are the items that *must* be within easy reach—and not necessarily the items that were previously close by. Analyze the form and function of your workspace, and assign each item its spot accordingly.

Probably the largest task will be reorganizing your filing system. This will also be the most rewarding task because, once you're finished, you'll be thrilled to see how much easier it is to find paperwork when you need it. You won't be slowed down by frantic searches for something that was "right here just a minute ago." You will know where each file is, and you will feel serene and calm as you reach for it.

Primary Home Office Clutter Zones

Clutter can rear its ugly head anywhere in your home office—squelching your potential for business success at every turn. It's difficult to pinpoint precise clutter zones, since your home office could be anywhere in your home (from a small corner of your kitchen to a spare bedroom or an addition to your home).

Despite the many variances in home office layouts or locations, clutter can pile up in several familiar places:

- **Behind doors.** Is there clutter behind Door #3? One sensible solution might be a hanging file rack on the back of the door. Just be sure to clean it out once in a while.
- **Alongside or on top of file cabinets.** Cabinets can become burial grounds for old files, leaving important new ones stranded. Doesn't it make sense to archive the older ones in cold storage and neatly store your current and active files?
- **On top of the desk and credenza.** This is where the "stack and spread" phenomenon begins. Instead of piling, you should be filing.
- **Under the desk and credenza.** You're busy working on the Great American Novel, and you just can't walk away from your desk to put away the mail or

background files. So, you pile them under your desk. Soon you've got a week's worth of clutter-removal to handle. Deal with it at the end of each day, before you're too tired or distracted by other tasks.

- **In your briefcase.** Since they represent your mobile office, briefcases need free-flowing chi, too. Stuffing your briefcase so full of papers that you need to sit on it to close it signifies insecurity and indecision. Decide which papers to take with you and which are okay to leave behind (or, better yet, pitch or recycle).

- **On chairs (or under them).** Chairs are for sitting, not for storing. If the extra chairs in your office are filled with books and papers, ask yourself what purpose this serves. Is it to keep others from intruding on your personal workspace? If so, look for other ways to create more natural boundaries for the peace you crave.

- **On windowsills.** Windowsills can be lovely, especially when they are permitted to let in the flow of air (and positive chi). Problems arise when you allow them to become an extension of your cluttered desktop.

The bottom line when dealing with clutter zones in your home office is to stay on top of the problem before it becomes a real problem—be decisive and honest with yourself about those objects that bring you peace and prosperity versus those that merely take up space. If it isn't serving you or your business, out it should go!

Avoiding the "Stack and Spread"

As you determine the appropriate place for everything in your office, beware of the "stack and spread" syndrome. You probably already know about this phenomenon: You figure that having a neat stack of files on your desk, along with a tidy pile of business magazines and other periodicals, is okay. Your main work area is completely cleared off; you place these piles of files on the far corner of the desk, out of the way, so the desk is tidy, right? Wrong!

Eventually, stacks end up becoming disorganized 'office-wreckers. It becomes a longer and longer process just to figure out if a file you need is even in the pile. Worse yet, over time the stack grows perilously high, putting it in danger of being knocked off the edge of the desk—and into oblivion. And, if you allow yourself one stack, you'll soon have several more, which will then spread into each other. The result, over time, is utter chaos. So, beware the "stack and spread" syndrome!

Clearing Space—and Your Mind

The first step is to recognize that you don't have to keep those files on your desk. Doing so, for most people, is a sort of security blanket. It's as if putting the files away in the file drawer makes them forever inaccessible. Not true. Having them neatly arranged in the proper place makes a space for "good" energy in your office. It also will reduce your stress level, because those piles of clutter create anxiety in your mind, preventing you from working effectively . . . and blocking the optimum feng shui environment.

Are you in panic mode after reading those words? If your mind is screaming, "But I *have* to keep files on my desk!" then read on.

 ESSENTIAL

E-mails, voice mails, and regular mail can quickly pile up if you allow them to get out of control. Answer each as soon as you can, or they will not only fill your desk, but also your mind, as worries over whom you've answered and whom you've ignored take on a life of their own in your head.

It isn't the piles themselves that create negative energy; it is having piles of papers and files that just sit there, untouched, for weeks on end that is the issue. This creates negativity in your office, and in your mind. It clogs the free flow of chi through and around your office. It wastes precious time—and time, as you know, is money in the business world. If the piles are frequently assessed, with some papers or files being removed from the desk and others replacing them, you'll avoid the negative energy. Have a policy of keeping different projects in separate file folders. Make a point of going through the piles each day, moving nonessential items from the desk to the filing cabinet or recycle bin as often as possible.

File It—or Pitch It

For everything else, establish a simple "file it or pitch it" policy. This sounds easy—and it is—but it requires absolute consistency if you want to succeed. From the moment an item enters your office, you need to control its placement. Create a file for it (and place it in the filing cabinet), pitch it, or put it in a project stack or "read me" stack (but again, don't let the stacks get static). Establish a specific time of day and day of the week at which to review any items in the "read me" stack. Make sure the "projects" files are reviewed daily.

If you cannot bear to throw something out, create a "temporary" file. Mark your calendar or Palm Pilot for a specific date each month, on which you will review everything in the "temporary" file. No item should remain in that file for longer than one month. It should be assigned to a file and put away, or pitched. Be ruthless about this: File it or pitch it! The successful flow of energy in and around your office depends on it.

Harnessing the Power of Feng Shui

Now that we've handled the basic decluttering, it's time to adjust your work setting to reflect proper feng shui.

Keeping those files put away, as mentioned, is important to allowing chi to work freely. So is keeping trash containers empty. But "poison arrows" must also be dealt with in order to bring positive chi flow to your home office. If you have books on your shelves, don't have them lined up in military precision; have some lying on their sides in small stacks and intersperse a few knickknacks or small plants among them. You can also push books to the front of shelves to soften their hard edges. This will redirect the "poison arrows" of negativity, and help you to keep that chi flowing in the direction you will find most useful in your entrepreneurial pursuits.

"Desked" for Success

Positioning yourself for success in your home-based business, in feng shui terms, has everything to do with auspicious, clutter-free positioning of objects and furniture in the room. Some experts state that your desk should be positioned in the corner diagonally opposite the door so that you can see who enters. If this isn't possible, you would do well to hang a small mirror over your desk so that you can see the door behind you reflected in it. The fame area would also be the optimal place for diplomas and certificates to be displayed.

The wealth and prosperity segment of the bagua is adjacent to the fame area. You might want to hang a small Chinese coin (preferably on a red ribbon) in this area to attract wealth. A jade plant would also enhance your wealth section, as would wind chimes or flags.

The knowledge and self-cultivation area would be a good place for books, tapes, and study materials. The career area would be enhanced by water symbols—a small water fountain, perhaps, or a mirror, glass, or small crystals.

Other areas of the bagua, though they may seem nonbusiness related, might have special meaning in your home office. In these areas, you can bring good chi into the office by strategically placing one or two symbolically lucky objects. For instance, in your helpful people corner, you might have a statue of an angel or a gift from a business mentor or benefactor. In the health corner of the room or desk (which, by the way, is generally located in the middle), you might place a small, yet healthy plant to symbolize your healthy business.

 ALERT

> Consider colors when decorating your home office. Lack of color can deplete energy before you even start working—however, too many competing colors in the room is a form of clutter and can create an atmosphere of extreme distraction.

Making a Deal with Clutter

By now, you probably recognize that one of the most harmful aspects of clutter is the fact that seeing stacks and piles of messy documents everywhere you look drains your energy. You will likely feel anxious and out of control when surrounded by mounds of messy paperwork, and it stands to reason: If everything around you is out of control, you will eventually *feel* out of control (and might even catch yourself saying it to friends and colleagues).

The old saying, "Out of sight, out of mind" is a feng shui truism—and in this case, it's very positive. If your work area is tidy, energy can flow freely. When energy flows freely, your creativity and concentration are optimized. And when that happens, your performance is at its peak. Now, that's a home office that means *business*.

Chapter 13

Clutter in the Workplace

lutter makes us uneasy. It scatters our attention and saps our energy. In the workplace, clutter is responsible for a tremendous loss in productivity. More and more effort is spent working around the outdated stacks of papers and reports that we save, or looking for that one important letter that actually we really do need. Over time, this impacts the company's bottom line, because, as we all know, time, in a very real sense, is money.

Cluttered Desks Speak Volumes

Picture in your mind the most cluttered desk you've ever seen (maybe even your own). It may have sticky notes stuck all over the phone, computer monitor, and lamp. It no doubt has untidy piles of file folders and paperwork stacked precariously on every corner. There may be postage stamps and phone message slips falling off the edge of one of the piles or invoices (or even checks) strewn haphazardly across the work surface (with a very "elderly" banana acting as a paperweight). There could be family photos, obscured by memos or covered with dust, and bulging "in" and "out" baskets.

Got that picture in your mind? What does it say about the person who uses that desk? If you are a business owner or manager and the desk is an employee's, it might send the message that the employee is careless about his or her work. It may say that this person can't be trusted with larger projects or more responsibility, because the chaotic workstation implies that the employee is undisciplined and unorganized.

Imagine that you're a coworker of the "messy desk maven." What message does the untidiness convey? You might question how you could work effectively with this person—after all, wouldn't he or she always be looking for missing files or memos? Wouldn't she lose any paperwork you entrusted to her? Wouldn't she miss deadlines?

And what if the clutter queen (or king) is . . . you? You probably feel out of control much of the time. You may feel that you simply can't cope, that you will never get caught up with your work. All too often, you may feel "out of kilter," unmotivated, even tired or irritable.

 ESSENTIAL

> Coping with clutter saps your energy, decreases your productivity, and sabotages your career success. It can ruin your confidence, creating a vicious cycle: You can't find key documents you need, or you miss deadlines because you buried your Palm Pilot in the rubble.

Clutter in your workplace causes you to fall behind in your work, so you suffer anxiety over being late. Next, you scramble to find the files you need to complete the late project, feeling inadequate all the while. Then, coming full circle, you find yourself stuck again, more and more behind in your work, and more worried and frazzled.

But it doesn't have to be that way. Using the principles of feng shui as a guide, you can change your messy habits. You can stop the cycle and get back on top of your game.

Clearing Your Path to Success

One of the benefits of feng shui is that it can be used to create pathways. In this sense, it can be a new road map to guide your thinking and your work habits up the ladder to career success.

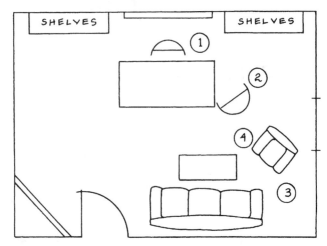

Office Survival Plan: This plan works because it limits potential for clutter. You can use the bookcases behind your chair, from where you can see the door, yet are not directly facing it (1). The desk's guest chair is in the desk's wealth/health segment (2). Guest seating in the helpful people corner facilitates easy conversation (3), and the single armchair still has a good view of the door (4).

For example, don't clutter the career bagua area of both your desk and your entire office with furniture, books, and piles of files. This will literally bury your career—and it will be a huge red flag to your supervisor, especially come promotion time. As a rule of feng shui in business, you never want to create negative energy that hinders your own path to prosperity—and it's political suicide in the workplace to be known as a clutter magnet.

Also, you should keep the helpful people area of your bagua open to mentoring possibilities. The clearer you keep this area, the more open you obviously are to coaching, mentoring, or inspiration from your colleagues. The more cluttered the helpful people section of your desk or office is, the louder you're telegraphing how closed you are to suggestion, coaching, or ideas from others. Though these messages come across on a subliminal, unconscious level, you should realize that the more closed you seem to input from others, the less of a chance you'll have to move ahead when opportunity knocks. Remember that part of mindfulness is remaining open to the flow of new ideas. Show respect to your colleagues by keeping your helpful people area open for positive exchanges.

Clutter Hotspots on Your Agenda

From a career standpoint, clutter is not limited to your desk. It can be everywhere from floor to ceiling, depending on how high the stack of "unmade decisions" rises. Here are some other clutter zones in the workplace:

Floors

The "stack and spread" can happen quickly. Within a few weeks, the piles can move and spread until your colleagues feel like they're parting the Red Sea every time they need to ask you a question. From a feng shui standpoint, piles on the floor slow the chi to the point of stagnant energy.

Cubicle Walls

These can be literally covered in family photos, posters with silly sayings, theatre tickets, and all kinds of other paper clutter. Be mindful in what you share with others—your cubicle can literally be the window to your soul. Choose a few significant items and leave the rest at home.

Filing Cabinets

These can be filled with too many ancient files that should be archived in cold storage. Use the cabinets for current files, and you'll be able to stay on top of "file pileup." Files should be able to move, and not be jam-packed so that you get a paper cut every time you go looking for the latest P&L statements!

Credenzas and Drawers

Are yours so stuffed with paper that the cabinets or drawers won't even close? Are they still important to you? If not, remove them, along with all of those old paper clips, pens that have outlived their usefulness, and old, brittle rubber bands.

Bookshelves and Windowsills

Bookshelves can be overloaded with items from your past—old magazines, journals, textbooks, papers, and the like—that may holding you back from your future potential. Instead, consider one new item (such as fresh flowers) on your windowsill, and several helpful resources on your bookshelves. To maximize the helpfulness of your reference books, consider placing the bookshelves in the knowledge corner of your office.

Conference and Lunch Rooms

Wherever large groups of people meet, there exists a potential for clutter. Food can be left out for long periods of time, garbage can be left unattended, and company refrigerators allowed to accumulate moldy, disgusting food specimens. If you walk by a situation like any of these, be part of the solution—toss it out! Send a memo around that unclaimed food will be tossed every Friday.

Computers

Do you get frequent reminders from your computer that your e-mail box is full, or that your hard drive is nearly full? Clutter can accumulate everywhere on your computer, but especially in cache files that you don't really need. Delete unnecessary messages and files—and store useful-yet-old files on a disk, CD, or zip drive.

 ESSENTIAL

Before feng shui's wonderful harmony can be set free in your work area, you have to make room for it. It will be well worth the effort, because you will feel more and more empowered, more and more energized, with every step you take in the direction of clearing that pathway to success!

The Image of Success

Think about the messages you're sending to others, and perhaps give even more thought to the reasons behind your need for clutter. Did the metaphoric "snapshot" of the typical messy desk open your eyes to how an untidy desk can sabotage your career success? If that eye-opener didn't do the trick, just open any business magazine and see how much print is given to the importance of organizing your workspace. So, isn't it time to create a pathway for "good chi" (energy) in your work-related surroundings?

The first step is to declutter. Start by removing everything from the top of your desk. Everything! Notice that you're already breathing more easily and feeling less stressed—just from taking that one tiny step.

Next, carefully consider what *should* be permitted in your work area. First, put the phone, computer, and lamp back on the desk. Don't concern yourself too much with placement at in the beginning of this exercise. Next, think through your workday: What items are essential to a typical day? Odds are, this will include such things as a clock, a stapler, pens/pencils, sticky notes, paper, and paper clips.

Take a step back (perhaps both literally and metaphorically). See your desk through the eyes of others that see it each day. What is the image you want them to form about you and your work habits? Make sure your desktop matches the image and goals you have in mind.

Taming the Paper Monster

Now, the tricky part: You need to *ruthlessly* assess the remainder of items that you removed from your desk. We can be quite certain that *all* of them do not need to go back onto your desk. But do *any* of them need to reside there? Can they instead be stored in a file nearby? Should they be relegated to a cabinet or credenza? Remember, you've just cleared a pathway on your desk for success, and you don't want all the energy to get clogged up in piles of material that belong elsewhere.

That brings us to the dreaded "paper monster." Paper is the biggest mess-maker in your office—and the hardest monster to tame. But tame it you must. You deserve the opportunity to give full rein to your talents and skills so that you can experience prosperity of every kind, and for that you need the right atmosphere—serene, positive, and energized (as opposed to anxious, overwhelmed, and indecisive). Your office must encourage free-flowing, "good chi"—strong and yang—to meet your goals.

 ESSENTIAL

> As you go through the piles that had been on your desk, discarding as many items as possible, notice the stagnant energy that surrounds them. Visualize the strong, "now-we're-getting-somewhere" type of energy that will soon replace it.

It may be hard to examine the chaos, but this is essential to creating a functional, balanced work area. If you do need to retain an item, analyze the form and function of your workspace, and assign each item its spot accordingly. Determine what the most appropriate place for it might be. Does it need to be in reach of your desk? Do others need access to it? How often do you use it? Don't "overthink" these decisions; just assume that if it has to be saved at all, it has to have a "home" somewhere other than on your desktop. File it, box it up, recycle it, or stack it on a closet shelf. (Note: Beware of simply stuffing things in drawers or closets. Even "hidden" messes will have a negative impact on the energy in your workspace.)

 ESSENTIAL

Set a weekly appointment for clearing your "in" basket. For instance, at the end of the day on Friday, you might clear your files so that your desk will be clear and ready for new challenges on Monday. This will give you a fresh perspective as you begin a new week.

Don't get discouraged. Take frequent breaks and reward yourself for your progress. Take it one moment at a time, one section or project at a time. The trick is to be *decisive*. Remember, if you haven't touched some files for over a year, they can be archived in a faraway place, somewhere other than your office.

Of course, by the time you've gotten all the junk that was on your desk sorted out, filed, tossed, or archived, you will realize that (gasp!) the file cabinet, closet, etc., will need to be reorganized. This is a big task, but break it down into "do-able" chunks. Your reward will be seeing how much easier it will be to find the materials you need quickly. Frantic searches for missing paperwork will be a thing of the past. You will know where each file is, and you will feel serene and calm as you reach for it.

Getting Rid of Computer Clutter

Like a desk full of files and paper clutter, your computer can easily become a wasteland for all that you are working on. Just because you can't see it doesn't mean it's not stored somewhere in the vast archives of your hard drive. In fact, every time you visit a page on the Internet, your cache file stores an impression of the page until the day you go in and clean up the residual.

Don't wait until your hard disk sends you an S.O.S. Read through your files and messages and decide in real time whether you're going to store or delete each one. Do it a little bit at a time, several times a day, and soon you'll be on clutter-control autopilot!

What about all those "critical" files that you absolutely can't delete? For these, you should develop a filing system that is intuitive enough to help you quickly identify such files as you need them. For instance, just as you have an "in" basket on your desk, you might also consider having an "in" file in which you temporarily place all of the files you are currently working on. When these projects are complete and you are ready to move the files to an archive, create a system that is intuitive. In other words, with folder names that are easily identifiable once you start searching through the archives to find a file you may have created and saved more than a year ago. For files older than a year, consider developing a folder system that is organized first by year, then by project name. This will help keep you organized and productive, and will alleviate the clutter of worry in your own "hard drive"—your brain!

 ALERT

> To keep your computer hard drive from getting overloaded when you have lots of files to store, add a zip drive to your computer and do regular backups to your system. This will also help prevent data loss should your system crash.

Creating a Prosperous Future

Time for the most crucial step of all: As soon as you've decluttered and reorganized your workspace, you need to *immediately* form new habits to replace the old ones. Otherwise, you will end up with the same ugly, disorganized paper stacks, old bananas, and dirty coffee cups that caused all the problems in the first place!

Jot down some simple notes—rules, if you will—for what can/cannot be on your desk. Create a process that will help you consistently and easily deal with incoming mail, phone messages, and e-mails. Describe how you will handle incoming projects and the paperwork that goes with them. Set a policy of handling papers only once: Read it, file it, pitch it, or pass it along to someone else. Consider everything that crosses your desk as a "hot potato" that requires some sort of action. Re-read your new organizational "rules" every day, at least at first, until your new habits begin to feel ingrained.

Now it's time to look at your office with "best feng shui practices" in mind. Keeping those files and piles off your desk, as mentioned above, is important to allowing chi to work freely, as is keeping trash containers empty. Include small objects or plants on your bookshelves to break up the regular lines of books standing at attention.

 ALERT

Remember that piles of work create negative energy, causing you stress, low self-esteem, and a lack of confidence. Don't clog the free flow of chi through and around your office. It wastes precious time and money.

If you want to lift any stagnant energy on your desk, bring in some fresh flowers and place them in a lovely vase! They will raise the energy level in the room (or cubicle), while brightening your attitude. If possible, find ways to bring sunlight to your workspace; it heralds warmth and yang energy. You can accomplish this with mirrors, reflective glass on framed pictures, and lamps with full-spectrum lighting that mimics daylight. Notice the placement of symbols and objects in the room. Ideally, you should face south (this is the fame area), with your back to the wall, for support. The fame area is also the optimal place for diplomas and certificates to be displayed. The southern direction is also associated with increased sales—something that will be important to those in sales, marketing, or operations.

Be careful in your mindful placement of helpful items not to go overboard—too much of a good thing can spoil your chances for success by choking the chi in your office space.

Remember, your attitudes, the placement of objects in your office, and the containment of clutter are keys to your career success. Your work area should support your goals in life.

If it pays homage to feng shui principles and symbols, if it is tidy, clean, and well organized, you will be calm and confident. Energy will flow freely, so that your creativity will be optimized. And when that happens, you will operate at peak performance. What more could you want?

Chapter 14

The Clutter Inside

Between the 10,000 or so thoughts, decisions, dreams, and plans you've got rolling around in your head at any moment are the real or imagined worries that keep you up at night. "I've got too much on my mind," you say, not realizing just how true that really is. Even if you establish outer harmony in every space of your home, it will do you little good without harmony within yourself. Indeed, the space in your head is the final frontier in feng shui decluttering.

A Head Full of Clutter

On the average day, we carry a lot with us in our minds—everything from our grocery lists to vacation dreams and grandiose plans for the future. We go from idea to idea, sometimes without any logic whatsoever, as rapidly as wildfire, and then wonder why we can't remember where we left our car keys. It's no wonder that stress builds a nest in our minds, a worry-filled place where all the neurons are under constant attack from every direction.

You know the gut-wrenching syndrome: "Did I remember to lock the doors to my home? Are my pets going to be okay while I'm on vacation? Do you think I hurt her feelings by saying that? Should I have invited so-and-so to lunch?" You can really send yourself on a daily guilt trip with questions and worries like these self-esteem-based concerns.

If you're a real worrywart, try making a weekly (or, if you're really bad, daily) appointment with yourself to vent, worry, or obsess over whatever comes to mind at the time. Write it all down in a journal or on a piece of paper you burn at the end of your "worry session." Adding the fire element will help you to break up the negative energy of too much worry, freeing you from the clutter it so easily creates in your mind.

When we don't deal with things quickly enough, we allow them not only to stay as unwelcome visitors, but also to burrow deeply within our minds on a more permanent basis. How can we free ourselves from never-ending worry and stress? We can start by removing the baggage of excessive thought—by clearing our minds of the mental clutter that has piled up over weeks, months, and often years. Such purging requires a commitment to trying several different methods until finding one that works best; for some, meditation is the answer; for others, physical exercise is the best way to alleviate mental clutter. The point is to keep at it until you figure out the key to breaking the cycle of pain—and fear.

 ESSENTIAL

It is often said by psychologists that anger is fear turned outward. When you can figure out what you're afraid of, you can break the cycle of poor self-image and excessive mental clutter. Try journaling to get to the bottom of your fears.

The Fear Factor

Just knowing that there are clutter "dust bunnies" running around in your head at any given moment is not really enough to start dealing with them on a long-term basis. You need to look at the fear behind the clutter—and that fear can take many different forms.

Most obvious is the fear of letting go. If you have lots of mementos from your past, but never look at them or use them, you likely have a fear of letting go of these things. No doubt, behind that fear is a difficulty in moving forward toward the future. Are you stuck in the past, or afraid of an uncertain future? It's okay to admit that your piles of clutter represent a fear of moving forward, as long as your next step is to remove these "pillars of the past." Your memories are safe in your mind and heart—you don't need an attic full of "artifacts" to prove you had a past.

Living Up to Expectations

You may be afraid of living up to new expectations as a result of your newfound ability to effectively deal with clutter. What will they expect from you after you finally get rid of 75 percent or more of your possessions? In this sense, it's kind of like losing weight: As soon as others begin to notice the change, the pressure to continue the program mounts. Can you live up to their expectations? This could be a major worry for you, especially if you're not fully committed to long-term change yet. You don't want to be seen as weak, but you may not be ready to make any big decisions for a clutter-free future, either. Such ambivalence can easily lead to more procrastination than ever in the future if you're not careful.

Finally, you may have a fear of making decisions in the first place. What will you do if the next decision you make isn't a good one? What will people think? What if your first answer wasn't really the correct one on that test? What if you're flat-out wrong about a situation at work? When you consider the sheer volume of decisions we have to make on a daily basis, it's easy to see how the law of averages comes into play: The chances of our being right more than 50 percent of the time are very slim. So what if you choose incorrectly? Unless lives are at stake, you will emerge from the bad decision a wiser, healthier person.

Don't get stuck in the inertia (and constricted chi) of negativity about the decisions you face on a daily basis. You'll be right sometimes and wrong others, but the most important lesson of all is in the journey of self-exploration, as you learn from the good and bad experiences that make up your life.

Are Your Decisions Making Themselves?

Left to their own devices, your decisions will start to make themselves in time. That vacation you were putting off will become impossible because you didn't request the appropriate time off. That fabulous dinner at the gourmet restaurant doesn't happen because you couldn't decide when to plug it into your busy schedule. Those clothes that didn't fit anymore exploded from your overstuffed closet. On their own, each episode of indecision may seem innocuous, but add them all together in a short period of time and you wind up looking extremely insecure about yourself.

Who is really in control here—you or the things and ideas that you own? Do you really enjoy waiting until something absolutely must be done about a situation before taking any positive action to move things along? Whether they are large or small in scope, unmade decisions can create a sense of inertia for you, leaving you with lots of stagnant chi and keeping you off the path to your greatest potential. For good feng shui, you have to have the upper hand in all of your personal decision-making. Imagine how good it will feel to be making good choices in real-time—and allowing yourself the opportunity to make (and learn from) mistakes along the way. What a gift!

 ALERT

> Be careful about leaving too many things to chance. While the Chinese believe that some things are best left to nature, they also believe in responsibility, cause, and effect. You alone control your destiny—and there's no better way to achieve your goals than to set and follow the path for yourself.

Inner Space Clearing

Getting clear in your head is not only a goal in feng shui, it's also the main objective in yoga and Zen meditation. But how can you accomplish "inner nirvana" by creating a peaceful oasis in your mind?

You needn't become a Buddhist monk to learn the art of clearing your mind for your greater good. Inner clearings can be achieved in the following simple, inexpensive, and practical ways that won't cramp your need for socializing.

Meditation

Using deep breathing, visualization, and chanting can be an extremely effective way of clearing mind clutter. Find a quiet, comfortable place in your home, and make sure you won't be interrupted for at least an hour. Some people choose to go to a gym for meditation classes—a great idea if you're a novice, but eventually it's even better to create a "mind spa" in your own home.

Yoga

Even though it's along the lines of meditation, yoga focuses more on the mind-body connection in meditation; this can involve your entire body in the clutter-removal process. A great way to get the clutter out—and the blood flowing!

List Making

Putting it all down on paper can really help you to remove the more menial tasks from your mind—and can help you stay on top of all your life's details. Be realistic in your list making by not including too many tasks for each day. Pencil in some breathing time between projects.

Music

Across diverse cultures and throughout many time periods in history, music has been used to improve the lives of the suffering. So imagine what it can do for a little clutter in your mind. Put on whatever works for you, whether it's classical, rock, jazz, or rhythm and blues.

Relaxation Techniques

Deep breathing and visualization, for example, can be quite helpful in mentally "dissolving" that which is consuming your thoughts. You can use these in tandem with yoga or meditation, or on their own throughout the day. You can even schedule a "Zen moment" in the middle of the afternoon at work to catch a few cleansing breaths.

 FACT

When you free your mind of clutter, you will also open the channels to your intuition. One of the benefits of a clear mind is that it is highly receptive to psychic and spiritual input from a higher source.

Empathic Mind Clutter

Your best friend calls with a problem, which you don't mind trying to solve at 11:30 P.M., the night before your big presentation to the boss. "It's okay," you say to your-self, "I can handle it." The next day rolls around, and you're very tired but ready to perform on the job, when a coworker approaches you with another personal problem. You endure the stress of doing a presentation without much preparation time—and then go to lunch with your coworker to help her solve her problem. On your way home from work, your friend calls again on your cell phone to go into part two of her continuing saga. "When did I become the psychologist for the world?" you ask yourself, half jokingly. The thing is, you have allowed yourself to absorb the problems of others around you—leaving yourself few precious moments to handle the harried details of your own life.

This kind of empathic mind clutter can fill up your life to the point where you wind up needing help from someone else to deal with all the negative energy you've sponged off of others—not a happy scenario for one as well intentioned as you.

 ESSENTIAL

Treat yourself to a "spa night," complete with a bubble bath, candles, and some soft music. Allow your mind to wander freely, and celebrate all the good you do for others on a regular basis. Acknowledge that you're worthy of good as well!

If you are an emotional sponge, internalizing all of everyone else's problems, you are letting down the most important person of all: yourself. While you're busy solving the world's problems, your own needs have been piling up everywhere around you. In your living room, den, or bedroom, your clutter is a visible sign of your neglect of the inner you. How could you have allowed this to happen?

Go easy on yourself. Recognize that while it may be good to help others, you can't take on the burden of their problems. Their problems are theirs to carry, and ultimately theirs to deal with as well. You can offer advice and support where needed, but when push comes to shove (and it often does in these situations), you will need to let go of your need to fix things for others and focus your attention on your own energy. In the end, you can only be as good to others as you are to yourself.

Turn Down the Volume

You're sitting in your sacred new clutter-free space, your mind free from all of the empathic and fear-based clutter that once held it hostage. Taking a slow, deep breath, you put on a little music in your living room for some relaxing time to stretch and read a good book on your sofa, when all of a sudden you hear your son's CD player blasting from his bedroom. Your daughter's instant messaging on the computer with her best friend at the same time she's arguing on the phone with her boyfriend. You move outside to the patio, and just as you begin to relax once more, your husband decides it's the perfect time to mow the lawn.

Like the worry that previously consumed your thoughts and took up valuable space in your brain, noise clutter can consume you in a New York minute. In a society inundated with more home entertainment options than ever, we can quickly move from total silence to boisterous activity that rivals that of the Osbournes.

Simple solutions, such as creating a family rule of only one source of noise at a time, can help to keep peace in your head—and also in your home. But being mindful and creative at the same time can also do the trick. For instance, if you're writing a report and your computer happens to be in the same room as an all-important baseball game on television, ask the sports fan to consider using the "closed caption" feature on the TV while you are busy typing away. Or purchase headphones for your children to listen to their music more quietly in their rooms. Often, we're so afraid of upsetting or offending anyone else that we allow him or her to offend us with unsettling amounts of noise. But if you don't defend your peace and quiet, no one else will. Stand your ground—and quiet your mind for the rest, relaxation, and rejuvenation it needs to keep your soul healthy.

 ESSENTIAL

> Remember the universal law of prosperity: What you put out into the Universe is what you will get back. Do you want greater abundance in all things? Your own positive, prosperous attitude is the real starting point.

Staying in the Decluttering Mindset

Once you have finally mastered the ability to clear the clutter in your mind—and protect it from further clutter—

you will have developed a stronger sense of self in addition to a feng shui-based "decluttering mindset." Nothing will be able to interfere with your new way of thinking, except previous bad habits that may cause a temporary relapse. Still, over time and with regular practice, you can learn to stay focused on your healthier new frame of mind, lessening the noise all around you. Now that you are as aware of your inner environment as your outer, you can move toward the final step of staying clutter-free forever.

Chapter 15

Curing Clutter Issues for Good

Bringing harmony and balance to your surroundings is the essential first step to having a clutter-free home full of positive energy. But removing clutter issues from your life for good involves a long-term commitment and a willingness to look within for the reasons behind the clutter. To stay on top of the "mound of indecision," which is a more accurate emotional description of clutter, you should be continually focused on clearing the chi that surrounds you.

Healing Your Excess Baggage

Healing the baggage created by excessive inner and outer clutter is not an easy task—at least not at first. Like any other emotion-based form of release, you will need to look deeply inward for any long-term solution to become possible. In this sense, recovery from repeated patterns of clutter is much like any other habit-breaking program.

The first step toward positive change is admitting to yourself that there is indeed a problem. This goes beyond the initial, "Gee, it's a little cluttered in here." It is more along the lines of the recognition that you are slowly becoming engulfed by your possessions. This awareness that there is a pattern to your life is the beginning of a more positive and lasting solution.

 ESSENTIAL

Clutter is about obstacles, and feng shui is about how to overcome obstacles. Think of yourself as your own "director of energy"— you alone control the flow of chi in and around you.

Next, you need to ask yourself whether you are ready to let go of your need for more things. Are you excessively needy? Are you insulating yourself with possessions to numb your pain about feelings of inadequacy or ambiguous self-worth? When will enough be enough?

Every time you consider a new purchase, ask yourself what need you are really seeking to fulfill. Sometimes, it truly is a practical purpose that you're serving, such as purchasing a ladder to remove tree-clutter on your roof. But if it's just something that you want because it's interesting or beautiful, ask yourself what you'd be willing to give up in its place, with the idea that you'll always try to keep the same amount of stuff.

As you already know from your life's history of dealing with it, clutter can literally follow you around, creating extra baggage for both you and your loved ones. But inside the baggage of your clutter you will find a ticket to a new, more positive life—one free of the challenges and obstacles that have, in the past, held you back from your true potential. Emptying out the baggage allows you to retrieve this ticket, and embark on a new life full of positive, life-enhancing chi energy. Don't be afraid to dig your way to this ticket, and to take the few extra steps to get back on the road to success.

Using Feng Shui Cures

Every time you make a change in your life or living environment, it changes the energy of space. Sometimes chi can get stuck in the middle of such changes, even if they are positive, healthy ones. To get the chi moving positively again in your environment, or simply to enhance what's already there, you can enlist the aid of any of the following symbolic elements that are considered to be effective "cures."

Crystals

These lovely room accents are actually powerful movers of chi, reflecting light and life to all points around them. In feng shui, crystals are considered transmitters of positive energy, making them ideal "cures."

 FACT

A crystal, when hung from a doorway, ceiling, or in front of a window, can catch sunlight and redirect it all over an otherwise stagnant room. When you hang a new crystal, be sure to mentally state your intention as you do so. It can be as simple a statement as, "I hang this crystal to increase the flow of positive energy in my home."

Mirrors

When a room is small, it can very easily appear cluttered—with only a few items actually in the room! Use mirrors when you want to lift energy or create an illusion of a larger room, but also when you want to reflect (or magnify, symbolically speaking) the most powerful corner of the room. For instance, you might want to emphasize wealth and prosperity in a small den or home office; here, you would do well to position a mirror to multiply the image of a clutter-free wealth corner of the room.

Fountains

Particularly in the money or career areas of the bagua in your home, you may want to intentionally place a small fountain to symbolize or attract prosperity. Be sure to keep this corner free from the outside influences of clutter, as "junk-energy" tends to confuse the positive energy generated by the free-flowing fountain. You don't want anything to get between you and your prosperity!

Symbolic Figures

Many Chinese restaurants feature a lucky cat or frog statue near their cash registers. These are considered to bring wealth. If you are experiencing the inner clutter of stress and worry, consider placing a Buddhist Quan Yin (goddess of mercy and compassion) statue in the corner of the bagua most relevant to the source of your stress. For difficulty pertaining to children, place Quan Yin in the family section of your home's overall bagua.

Wind Chimes

Sound is also a wonderful way to cure a space from its previous energy. Each time the wind catches the chimes, a new sound pattern is created—and a new energy results.

Plants

Living beings such as plants can act as energy buffers to the harmful rays of electromagnetic energy transmitted throughout your home. They can also balance out negative energy, particularly if you have lots of sharp corners in a room. Since plants have healthy and positive yang energy, they can counteract negativity from such sharp corners. If you use plants as a cure, just be sure to keep them healthy or they will lose their yang energy.

Pairs

Ever wonder how you can have all the things you ever wanted in your life, but still not feel like your relationship has what it needs? Perhaps you could pair specific items (such as candles) together in a clutter-free relationship corner of your bedroom. This could "ignite" lots of possibilities for togetherness!

Candles

Light energy is a fabulously romantic way of curing a stagnant space, especially after you've cleared it of clutter. As the flames flicker toward the ceiling, so goes your attachment to your old possessions, freeing you symbolically from the bonds of ownership. This is why candles can be an especially powerful tool in meditation.

Curing yourself of your feng shui woes is not only healthy, it's also necessary. Few of us has a home that's always in perfect balance with free-flowing chi all around. Besides, wouldn't some candles and wind chimes add a little much-needed romance to our lives?

Get It Going: Crystals are quick, easy cures for areas where the chi appears to be stuck. Round, multi-faceted ones work best; avoid hanging crystals with sharp edges.

Doing a Space Clearing

Throughout this book, the concept of space clearing has been mentioned several times. But what exactly is this feng shui practice—and how or when should a space-clearing ceremony be done?

Space clearing is the process by which old, stagnant residual energy is encouraged to redirect into healthy, free-flowing chi. It is the removal and replacement of unproductive energy with life-giving new energy.

When should you perform a space-clearing ritual? After removing clutter, to be sure, but also after you've experienced major life changes, or any other disruption in your living space (such as a fight with your children or spouse). Basically, you should do a space clearing anytime you experience the feeling that your room's energy has been brought to a screeching halt. Remember, the purpose of this ritual is to get the positive chi flowing again—and keep it moving freely!

 ALERT

> Beware of false feng shui cures! Many unscrupulous sellers (particularly on the Internet) will try to sell you "lucky" feng shui talismans that are really aimed at making them money, not at helping your situation. Consider the intention of the seller before offering your credit card number.

Items for Cleansing

There are items you can use to accomplish a space clearing in your environment, to clear it of the harmful rays of negative energy. First, make sure you are feeling healthy yourself, as you are the conduit of the newly created energy force. Meditation prior to a space clearing not only cleanses your soul before you begin, but it can also raise your vibrational energy level so that you are a more powerful conduit of positive energy.

Smudging with an herbal smudging stick is probably the most frequently used method of conducting a space clearing in your home. This method goes back in history to a time when smoke was used by Native Americans to purify land and belongings. You can either purchase smudge sticks at a metaphysical store or grow your herbs such as sage or rosemary for smudge sticks in your own garden. Once you've collected them, band them together with a string into a thick stick-like formation and light one end so that it burns like incense, emitting its scent as you walk through each room. Keep a small clay or metal dish handy to catch the ashes as you go. As you move through each room, mindfully state the purpose of each room and then walk clockwise through it, "blessing" each area of the room with its new clutter-free energy. If you wish, you can ask your spirit guides for assistance in this ritual.

Mineral sea salt, known by the ancient Greeks and Romans for its purification and restorative features, is also commonly used for space-clearing rituals. In fact, many Greeks still use it to ward off evil spirits! You can purchase sea salt at your local health food store. Wherever you intuitively sense that space needs to be cleared, you can sprinkle a small amount of this healing sea salt to energetically "lift" the chi in the space. Just one whiff of this rejuvenating mineral will lift your spirits as well!

Incense and other aromatherapy-related products can also lift energy and get it moving once again. Lavender is a preferred scent for its balancing effects on energy, and for that reason is often used in land healings as well. In fact, many metaphysicians and parapsychologists use lavender to make peace with spirits whose unrestful presence has been detected. Whatever scent you choose for a space clearing after decluttering, the best way to dissipate it into the air is by fire or water. If the scent is in incense or candle form, burn it to release the stagnant chi in the air; if you're using aromatherapy oils, mix them into a small spray bottle with some water. Spritz away negative energy in every corner of your home—and keep a little extra for yourself, since you've basically created your own perfume!

 ESSENTIAL

You should try to clear clutter regularly—but particularly after an illness or major change in your life. After you clear the clutter that may have resulted from a stressful period, do a space clearing to help clear negative chi—and to rid your home of harmful residual energy.

Quick and Peaceful Rituals

The fastest, easiest, and most practical method for space clearing is clapping your hands in the spaces where chi needs to get a move-on or where a clearing has been deemed necessary. This method is especially helpful immediately following an argument or minor disruption in the environment, but can also be "handy" as an "on-the-go" space-clearing ritual when decluttering.

Since space clearing is such a meditative activity, you might consider beginning and ending each space-clearing session with a meditation session at your altar or in your "sacred space." This will offer you the peace of knowing that each clearing has a beginning and an end, and that you can move on with your life with the full knowledge that you are doing your best to keep your opportunities in life wide open. What a great feeling!

Creating Sacred Space

Creating what feng shui practitioners refer to as "sacred space" is not limited to the practice of prayers with incense-filled altars. Ultimately, all of your living space should be sacred to you somehow. After all, each room serves a specific purpose in your life. Go through each room of your home and ask yourself, "What is this room's intention? What are my intentions with respect to this room—what do I most seek to create in this space?"

Ideally, your living space both serves and represents you. It shows the whole world who you are and what you believe in. Sacred space goes a step beyond—it nurtures the core of your soul. In sacred space, you feel your physical, psychological, and spiritual best—you are literally at one with all that is around you. Here, you find refuge and respite from the cold, cruel world—and the ability to reach within to find the source of rejuvenation that allows you to travel back outside again.

Sacred Space: Creating sacred space doesn't mean you have to have a candle-lit altar. Here is an example of a simple meditation area in a corner of a larger room. Note the symbolic angel wall sculpture, Indian picture, and natural reeds in a clay pot—a model of spiritual simplicity.

Getting Started

How do you create such a magical place in your own home? You do so first by identifying the best location for this kind of focus and introspection. Perhaps it's a dining room filled with angels and the images of other "helpful people." Or maybe it's a bathtub where you've created a spa-like escape complete with candles, mineral sea salts, and soft music. Where do you most see refuge when things go wrong? That is your first clue to a possible location for sacred space.

The second step of sacred space creation is to honor the space once you've designated it. Does this mean getting on your hands and knees and worshipping it? While you can certainly place spiritual "reminders" in this space, honoring it refers more to keeping it free of clutter, so that your intentions can stay focused and you can reflect on your life's potential without any outside interference. Here is the place you will come to for self-nurturing and a reconnection between the inner and outer you.

Everything in feng shui is energy-based and symbolic. If you fill your sacred space with things you no longer use or need, you are in essence sending the message to the Universe that you are comfortable with obstacles. Consequently, since the Universe mirrors back what we project outward, you will find yourself repeatedly faced with new obstacles and challenges strewn along your path.

Clearing the clutter when creating sacred space can be one of the most fulfilling aspects of feng shui—with the biggest psychological payoff. If you have a hard time letting go of some items that are in the way of sacred spaces, give them away to others who might find them meaningful—and bless them on their way out the door!

Making the Commitment

With the respect that you show each corner of each room comes the gut-level commitment to the well-being and purpose behind each. Long-lasting change won't happen until you add your willingness to commit to permanent solutions.

If you don't make a commitment to decluttering—and get support from other members of your family to keep up the momentum—you'll be back where you started in no time. Allowing the clutter to pile up again and again will only create more frustration and a source of constant stress.

Since decluttering is a powerful process that can remove negative obstacles from your life, it's no accident that it remains one of the most difficult chores in feng shui. Know that you are not alone in your struggle to gain control over it, and that there are many tools and resources that can help you stay on the path of good chi. One way to remind yourself of your commitment is to create sacred space zones in each of your rooms, with altars that allow you to give thanks to all who have helped you in your new endeavor.

 FACT

When you can finally achieve the clearing of space both physically and mentally, you will have also removed barriers to your higher goals. Just remember that, as goals change, needs change, and many items that served you before will no longer serve you on the road ahead.

Or, you may want to use a checklist to help you stay focused on clearing your clutter "hotspots" (see Appendix C for a checklist you can copy). If you need additional support, enlist the help of friends or relatives to help you stay on the "clutter wagon" for good. In many cases, they will secretly be relieved that you asked!

Relapses Happen

You've finally removed all of the clutter from your home, and it is now the peaceful oasis of which you've always dreamed. Clothes are neatly put away—with breathing space to spare—in your "closet Nirvana." The storage boxes are full of the things you have chosen to keep in your life, but out of the sight of others.

Then, almost without warning, it happens. Just when you've rid yourself of all of the excess knick-knacks, old makeup, and furniture that no longer serves you—just when you're on top of your own stress-free, clutter-free home—you begin to notice clutter piling up on the dining room table, or in the hall closet, or on your bedroom floor. "I'll get to that next weekend," you say to yourself—only next weekend becomes the next until several more months pass and suddenly you can't walk through your hallway anymore without stumbling over something. What have you done? You've allowed yourself to relapse.

Even if a relapse drags you back to that horrible place you were in the beginning of this book, you shouldn't feel defeated. Relapses happen—and, in fact, given your lifelong patterns of clutter-a-holism, they may well be expected along your path to more positive, lasting change.

Remind yourself of your commitment and purpose to clearing your surroundings of chi-inhibiting clutter. In the beginning, wasn't it about ridding yourself of the stressful feeling of being overwhelmed by, even choked by, your possessions? Weren't you spending a lot of time wondering whether you owned your possessions—or they owned you? Return to that place you were when you began the process of feng shui decluttering. Now think of how far you've come since that time. No doubt you've already made much of the positive progress that will help you stay on a clearer path to your future! A relapse here or there is not likely to keep you from this ultimate and worthy goal.

Stay mindful of what you want in your life and why you want it there. If and when relapses occur, always look within first for the answer as to why and how it happened. Forgive yourself. Then, get busy clearing the clutter—one more time! Allow yourself time to develop a pattern of clutter removal. Very few people are able to stay on top of things well the first time they try.

 ESSENTIAL

> When you've finished removing clutter after a relapse, you should always do a fresh space-clearing ceremony to remove the negativity of the previous clutter in the room. This is the feng shui way of room refreshening!

Clutter-free for Your Greater Good

Once you've developed a regular pattern of clutter clearing, you'll feel like a 10,000-pound weight has been lifted from your shoulders. Not only will your physical load be lighter, but your emotional and spiritual load will seem much more bearable as well. You'll be free, happy, and well adjusted—and secure in the knowledge that you can positively affect your own life. By clearing the things that no longer matter, you'll open yourself up not only for new possibilities and opportunities, but also for your ultimate, greater good.

With no more clutter in your life, you can experience the healthy flow of positive chi—the energizing life force of the Universe—all around you. But you can also become the inspiration for others who are seeking the same peace of mind that you've achieved. With all that you've done to clear the paths in and around your home, you'll have earned the title of "coach," remembering all the while, as author Richard Bach once said, that we teach best what we most need to learn.

Congratulate yourself on all the fantastic work you've done—for both your inner and outer environments!

Feng Shui Glossary

As you continue reading about feng shui practices, you will also continue to learn about related topics, religions, philosophies, and traditions. The following terms are used (and defined) in varying detail both in the text and in the glossary. For more in-depth information, please refer to any of several recommended feng shui resources.

"absent" space:

An area of the bagua that is not represented by a room in your home. It's also referred to in feng shui as a "missing" corner.

ancestors:

In Chinese culture, honoring ancestors is very important in maintaining good health and prosperity of the family. Ancestors are represented in the family corner of the bagua, which is on the middle left side of the octagon.

bagua:

An octagon representing the eight intentions of your life. It is used as an "energy" road map to help direct more positive energy to specific areas of your life. For instance, if you want to enhance your career, you could use the bagua to determine the career area of your home, then use the principles of feng shui to maximize your opportunities. In this sense, it can be a manifestation tool.

Black Hat Sect:

A school of feng shui that encourages one to rely heavily upon intuition. The only feng shui tool a Black Hat practitioner uses is the bagua.

Buddhism:

A school of spiritual thought based on the teachings of the Buddha, who believed that we all possess the ability to reach a state of Complete Understanding of nature, our lives, and the Universe. In Buddhism, enlightenment can be reached by releasing our earthly, mundane attachments in favor of higher spiritual thought. Much of feng shui (particularly in the Black Hat Sect) is based on the teachings of Buddhism.

career:

The area of the bagua that represents your career. Located in the front middle of the bagua. Most people enter their homes in the career sector of the bagua. Associated with the water element.

chi:

Often called qi. The invisible life force, or life energy, that the Chinese believe moves about in and around our bodies and environments.

children:

The area of the bagua that represents children and creativity. Located in the middle right area of the bagua. Associated with the metal element.

Chinese zodiac:

A popular and ancient method of astrology that explores the meanings, relationships, and synergies of twelve animal signs: rat, ox, tiger, rabbit, dragon, snake, horse, sheep, monkey, rooster, dog, and pig.

Compass School:

The Compass School of feng shui uses the compass to determine auspicious directions for energy. It is a highly intellectual versus intuitive school of feng shui thought.

Confucianism:

The teachings of fifth-century Chinese philosopher Confucius. These pearls of timeless wisdom refer mostly to moral conduct and ethical behavior.

cure:

When a negative position is encountered in feng shui, a cure can remedy the problem by reversing or redirecting the energy into a positive flow. For instance, if there is blocked chi in your doorway, you can hang a crystal to get the energy moving. There are eight basic remedies in feng shui.

destructive cycle:
Sometimes called the "reductive" cycle. Used to reduce the power of a dominating element. Each phase of this cycle reduces or minimizes the next phase.

dragon:
This animal of the Chinese zodiac represents east energy and the wood element.

earth element:
In feng shui, earth is one of the five elements that affect our lives. It is associated with relationships, resourcefulness, and earth colors.

east energy:
This energy propels us into action.

fame:
The area of the bagua that represents fame and reputation. Located in the rear middle of the bagua. Associated with the fire element and the color red.

family:
The area of the bagua that represents your family. Located in the front middle left side of the bagua. Associated with the colors blue and green.

feng shui:
The traditional Chinese system of placement, harmony, and balance within the environment. The goal of feng shui is to achieve harmony with chi, or the universal life force. Literally translated, *feng shui* means "wind and water," symbolic of the movement of energy.

fire:

Represents enlightenment and vision of self. One of the five elements, fire is associated with colors such as red and orange and with southern direction.

five elements:

In feng shui, there are five elements: earth, wood, metal, water, and fire. These are symbolic of the seasons and have both creative and destructive cycles.

five senses:

To achieve balance in feng shui, it is best to appeal to as many of your five senses (taste, touch, smell, sound, and sight) as possible in each room. Often, as we enhance a room's energy with items that appeal either visually, as with art, or to our sense of smell, as with potpourri, we forget that the other senses need attention as well. It's best to balance them in as many rooms as possible.

Form School:

The primary school of feng shui thought, based on the ancient Chinese need to maximize the lay of the land. Much attention is paid to topography of the land in this school of feng shui.

health:

The area of the bagua that represents the health of yourself and your family. Located in the center of the bagua.

helpful people:

The area of the bagua that represents the people who help you advance in your life. Located in the bottom right of the bagua. This is also commonly called the travel corner as well, and is associated with heaven and the colors white, gray, and black.

house blessing:

A ceremonial method of enhancing a space and endowing it with the strongest potential for good luck. Usually performed after a space clearing.

I Ching:

Ancient Chinese divination system, also known as the "Book of Changes." Much of feng shui theory is based on the I Ching.

intention:

An aim that guides an action and gives it purpose and meaning.

knowledge:

The area of the bagua that represents knowledge and self-growth. Located in the bottom left side of the bagua. The colors associated with the knowledge corner include black, blue, and green.

Lao Tsu:

Chinese philosopher credited with writing the I Ching, or "Book of Changes," on which much of feng shui is based.

luo pan:

This is the name given to the feng shui compass used to determine proper flow or direction of energy in your home or surroundings.

marriage:

The area of the bagua that represents marriage and important relationships. Located in the rear right corner of the bagua. This is the corner where you'd most want pairs of things, to symbolize love and partnership. Associated colors are red, pink, and white.

metal:
One of the five elements in feng shui. Metal represents structure and strength, but also creativity and recreation. Colors associated with the metal element include white, gold, and silver.

"mouth" of chi:
In feng shui, the main entrance to your home is considered the "mouth" or opening of chi. It allows energy to come in from the front door, then directs chi through your home.

mudra:
A series of symbolic postures and hand movements used in Hinduism to represent different stages along the path to enlightenment.

north energy:
In feng shui, energy from the north brings quiet, meditation, and stillness. Here, we can be introspective and nourish our selves.

phoenix:
A bird of great power, associated with southern energy and the fire element.

poison arrow:
Any sharp corner or straight object from which chi is bounced at an angle. If you have such a situation inside or outside your home, a feng shui cure is recommended, since poison arrows are considered to be bad luck or negative energy.

productive cycle:
In this cycle of the five elements, water nurtures wood, which feeds fire, which makes earth, which creates

metal, which holds water. Each phase of the cycle enhances the next.

qi:

Another spelling of *chi,* which is the invisible energy or life force that is within us and all around us.

qi gong:

Literally, "energy cultivation." Refers to exercises that improve health and longevity as well as increase the sense of harmony within oneself and in the world. There are thousands of such exercises.

smudge stick:

A tightly wrapped bundle of healing and spiritual herbs, used to clear or cleanse a space of negative energy.

snake:

Represents a central energy and is associated with the element of earth.

south energy:

Changeable, unpredictable, and enlivening energy.

space clearing:

In feng shui, a ceremonial method of removing negative energy in a room or structure and replacing it with a healthy flow of positive energy. Often involves walking through the structure with a smudge stick or lavender incense. A space clearing should be performed after any major change in the energy of a room (e.g., after an argument, redecorating, or remodeling).

tai chi:

The ancient Chinese practice of meditation in movement. Through a series of flowing movements and positions, tai chi has been proven to help lower blood pressure, and it promotes relaxation, harmony, and balance in mind, body, and spirit. In many ways, tai chi is like feng shui for the body, since it emphasizes fluidity of good energy or chi.

Taoism:

Sometimes called Daoism, this philosophy relies on intuition and the belief that we are one with nature.

tiger:

Associated with western energy and the metal element.

tortoise:

This animal in feng shui symbolizes the energy of the north and the water element.

trigram:

Most frequently associated with the I Ching, a trigram is a three-tiered set of broken and unbroken lines that symbolize the yin and yang that create all things and situations in life.

water:

Another of the five elements, water represents contemplation, reflection, and solitude. It is associated with blue, black, and the northern direction.

wealth:

The area of the bagua that represents wealth and prosperity. Located in the rear left corner of the bagua. This is where you might position your desk if you have a home office, or where you would hang a crystal to activate wealth energy in your home. Coordinating colors include blue, purple, and bluish red.

west energy:

Relaxing, creative yin energy.

white tiger:

Any tree, bush, building, fence, or landform located to the right of your home or business.

wood:

Represents growth, personal development, and the generation of new ideas or plans. Associated with green and the east. Wood is also one of the five elements.

yang:

Creative, dynamic energy. Often perceived as active and masculine energy. Yang and yin are complementary opposites.

yin:

Receptive, feminine energy that is seen by many as passive and soft. Yin and yang are complementary opposites.

Zen:

A movement of Buddhism that emphasizes enlightenment through meditation and intuition. The Black Hat Sect of feng shui relies heavily upon these principles.

Appendix B

Resources for Further Study

Now that you have decided to apply the principles of feng shui to your life, you may want to study the subject further. If you are interested in a deeper understanding of feng shui practices and Chinese wisdom, the following books, software, and feng shui organizations will help you to keep your intentions clear.

Books

Beattie, Antonia, with Rosemary Stevens. *Using Feng Shui* (Barnes & Noble, 2000). Nice, simple guide to the basic principles of feng shui.

Biggs, Jane Butler. *Feng Shui in 10 Simple Lessons* (Watson-Guptill Publications, 1999). Accessible guide with several question-and-answer sessions throughout. Very helpful to beginners.

Biggs, Jane Butler. *The Feng Shui Directory* (Watson-Guptill Publications, 2000). Handy guide divided with tabs by life intentions (health, wealth, career, etc.).

Brown, Simon. *Practical Feng Shui* (Ward Lock, 1997). Rich with diagrams and color photographs, this easy-to-understand book will help the novice to get started.

Carter, Karen Rauch. *Move Your Stuff, Change Your Life: How to Use Feng Shui to Get Love, Money, Respect and Happiness* (A Fireside Book, Simon & Schuster, 2000). Highly accessible and written in very modern, Western terms, this book is either loved or hated by anyone interested in feng shui. Still, it may be an easy way to get one's chi flowing in the right direction.

Chin, R. D. *Feng Shui Revealed: An Aesthetic, Practical Approach to the Ancient Art of Space Alignment* (Clarkson Potter, 1998). This book, with its lush photographs and captivating illustrations, offers a more detailed look at feng shui applications in very real settings.

Chuen, Master Lam Kam. *The Feng Shui Handbook* (Gaia, 1995). Simple guide to getting started with feng shui.

Chuen, Master Lam Kam. *The Personal Feng Shui Manual: How to Develop a Healthy and Harmonious Lifestyle* (Henry Holt & Company, 1998). Very accessible book that spends a lot of time sharing the nuances of Chinese wisdom (astrology, I Ching, etc.).

Collins, Terah Kathryn. *Home Design with Feng Shui* (Hay House, 1999). Colorful, easy-to-read book alphabetized and with tabs for easy reference. A great start!

Dexter, Rosalyn. *Chinese Whispers: Feng Shui* (Random House, 1999). Dexter designed this book herself, and it is a lovely work of art. But besides that, it also offers poetic glimpses into the wisdom and philosophy behind the art of feng shui.

Fontana, David, Ph.D. *Discover Zen: A Practical Guide to Personal Serenity* (Chronicle Books, 2001). Practical guide with rich, pastel illustrations that make you want to be more Zenlike in everything you do.

Gerecht, Hope Karan. *Healing Design: Practical Feng Shui for Healthy and Gracious Living* (Journey Editions, 1999). This well-organized and richly illustrated book offers plenty of food for thought not found in other books on feng shui.

Hale, Gill. *The Feng Shui Garden: Design Your Garden for Health, Wealth and Happiness* (Storey Books, 1998). Lovely photographs in this book make you wish you had a bigger yard—or more room to make a total feng shui statement inside and out. Recommended reading for feng shui followers with a green thumb.

Henwood, Belinda, and consultant Howard Choy. *Feng Shui: How to Create Harmony and Balance in Your Living and Working Environment* (Storey Books, 1997). Simple and easy to understand, this little guide will answer some basic questions about the practice of feng shui.

Hyder, Carole J. *Wind and Water: Your Personal Feng Shui Journey* (The Crossing Press, 1998). Lovely and spiritually uplifting book that offers wisdom for everything you are likely to do along your path on your feng shui journey. I love this book!

Karcher, Stephen L., and Rudolph Ritsema. *I Ching* (Element Books, 1994). Basic guide covering the history and wisdom of the I Ching.

Kennedy, David. *Feng Shui Tips for a Better Life* (Storey Books, 1998). Want to use feng shui to get more out of life? This book will be for you.

Kingston, Karen. *Clear Your Clutter with Feng Shui* (Broadway Books, 1999). A godsend for those who are bound by clutter.

Kingston, Karen. *Creating Sacred Space with Feng Shui* (Broadway Books, 1997). Inspiring guide to creating a space that matters versus placing matter in your space.

Lambert, Mary. *Clearing the Clutter* (Barnes & Noble,

2001). A great beginning guide for those just starting, but for more depth, see Karen Kingston's book on clutter.

Linn, Denise. *Feng Shui for the Soul* (Hay House, 1999). This book offers more of a metaphysical approach to feng shui, but it is a welcome and spiritually uplifting one, to be sure. I especially like the way Linn weaves ancestral energies into the feng shui mix.

Linn, Denise. *Sacred Space Clearing and Enhancing the Energy of Your Home* (Rider, 1995). Fantastic book about what it means spiritually to be rid of unwanted or negative energies.

Linn, Denise. *Space Clearing A-Z: How to Use Feng Shui to Purify and Bless Your Home* (Hay House, 2001). This A–Z guide features handy tabs to help you learn how to put the practice of space clearing to practical use. The house blessings are especially helpful.

Linn, Denise. *Space Clearing: How to Purify and Create Harmony in Your Home* (Contemporary Books, 2000). A terrific explanation of what space clearing is and how purification can bring about harmony in your home—and life.

Mah, Adeline Yen. *Watching the Tree: A Chinese Daughter Reflects on Happiness, Tradition and Spiritual Wisdom* (Broadway Books, 2001). This book contains a chapter or two on chi and feng shui, in the eyes of a Chinese woman who now lives in the Western world of California. Very insightful.

Post, Stephen. *The Modern Book of Feng Shui: Vitality and Harmony for the Home and Office* (Dell Publishing, 1998). This book offers a wealth of interesting tidbits about feng shui, and is suitable for the beginner.

Reid, Lori. *The Complete Book of Chinese Horoscopes* (Barnes & Noble, 1997). A colorfully illustrated guide to all the personality traits, characteristics, and compatibilities of each Chinese astrological sign. Great fun for the whole family.

Rossbach, Sarah, and Master Lin Yun. *Feng Shui Design: The Art of Creating Harmony for Interiors, Landscape and Architecture* (Viking/Penguin Putnam, 1998). A must for anyone interested in feng shui, especially the Black Hat Sect. Master Yun is the originator of that sect.

SantoPietro, Nancy. *Feng Shui: Harmony by Design* (Perigee Books, 1996). Very helpful book with plenty of real-life examples, including feng shui for the apartment.

Simons, T. Raphael. *Feng Shui Step by Step* (Crown Trade Paperbacks, 1996). From an informational standpoint, this book is helpful. The illustrations are very basic, however, and not as interesting.

Spear, William. *Feng Shui Made Easy* (Thorsons, 1995). Just what the title says it is, this book would be helpful to the uninitiated.

Stasney, Sharon. *Feng Shui Chic: Stylish Designs for Harmonious Living* (Sterling, 2000). This well-designed book, complete with its fabulous photographs of homes you wish you lived in, offers much in the way of concrete detail and real-life examples. One of the best books out there on the topic of modern feng shui.

Tan, Situ. *Best Chinese Idioms* (Hai Feng Publishing Company, 1986). Want to learn some of the famous Chinese sayings to impart their wisdom on your family and friends? Try this book.

Tanahashi, Kazuaki, and Tensho David Schneider. *Essential Zen* (Castle Books, 1994). Very insightful, interesting book on the practice of Zen meditation.

Thompson, Gerry. *Feng Shui Astrology for Lovers* (Sterling, 1998). Okay, so this is a little out of the feng shui realm—but you can learn a lot about what to put in your relationship corner if you want to attract a certain type. What's wrong with that?

Too, Lillian. *The Complete Illustrated Guide to Feng Shui Gardens* (Element Books, 1998). Beautifully illustrated and full of tips, this is an insightful book.

Too, Lillian. *The Fundamentals of Feng Shui* (Element Books, 1999). Full of cures, enhancements, and tips galore, this book will either be very helpful or put you into "feng shui overload" with the hundreds of things you can do to improve your life. My advice: Use the tips you need most now, and leave the rest for a time when you most need them.

Too, Lillian. *Lillian Too's Chinese Wisdom* (Cico Books, 2001). Fascinating guide to the history and background behind many Chinese traditions and pearls of wisdom.

Too, Lillian. *Lillian Too's Little Book of Feng Shui at Work* (Element Books, 1999). Handy guide to keep in your desk drawer for those spare moments when you can practice feng shui from your cubicle.

Too, Lillian. *Networking* (Element Books, 1997). Another great little feng shui book for business concerns.

Tsu, Lao. *Tao Te Ching* (Wildwood House Ltd., 1992). The Tao is essential reading for anyone interested in feng shui. It is one of the main foundations of this ancient practice.

Webster, Richard. *101 Feng Shui Tips for the Home* (Llewellyn, 1998). Helpful and full of great and practical tips.

Wei, Wu. *I Ching Wisdom* (Power Press, 1994). I just open this book daily to whatever it wants to teach me.

Wing, R. L. *The Illustrated I Ching* (HarperCollins, 1987). The I Ching is a wonderful Chinese divination tool, and this book makes it easy to implement it into your life.

Wydra, Nancilee. *Feng Shui for Children's Spaces: A Parent's Guide to Designing Environments in Which Children Will Thrive* (Contemporary Books, 2001). Accessible and easy to incorporate into your family's life, no matter how busy you are.

Wydra, Nancilee. *Feng Shui Goes to the Office*

(Contemporary Books, 2000). If I could only have one feng shui book in my office, this one would be it. A fantastic and helpful guide to implementing the practice of feng shui into modern, Western business.

Wydra, Nancilee. *Feng Shui: The Book of Cures* (Contemporary Books, 1993). Have problems with a missing corner in your living room? How about a front entrance with a straight path to the door? This book will prescribe the perfect feng shui antidote.

Organizations

Feng Shui Across America/Feng Shui Consultant Trainings
7609 New Utrecht Avenue
Brooklyn, NY 11214
Phone (718) 256-2640
E-mail: *nsanpietro@aol.com*

Feng Shui Guild
1919 8th Street, P.O. Box 850
Boulder, CO 80306
Phone (303) 444-1548

Feng Shui Institute International
7547 Bruns Court Canal
Winchester, OH 43110
Phone (614) 837-8370
Fax (614) 834-9760
E-mail: *fengshuimastersl@aol.com*
Web site: *www.fengshuiinstituteinternational.com*

The Feng Shui Institute of America
P.O. Box 488
Wabasso, FL 32970
Phone (772) 589-9900
Fax (772) 589-1611

Feng Shui Warehouse
P.O. Box 6689
San Diego, CA 92166
Phone (800) 399-1599 or (619) 523-2158
Fax (800) 997-9831 or (619) 523-2165
Web site: *www.windwater.com*

Worldwide Lin Yun Educational Foundation
205 De Anza Boulevard
San Mateo, CA 94402
Phone (650) 349-8868
Web site: *www.wlyef.org*

Yun Lin Temple
Feng Shui Master Lin Yun
2959 Russell Street
Berkeley, CA 94705
Phone (510) 841-2347

Software

Dragon Dance: A Guide to Life, Love, and Fortune Through Chinese Astrology. CD audiobook/reference booklet. Magnolia Films, 1999.

Feng Shui: Change Your Surroundings and Transform Your Life. CD-ROM. COMPUworks/The WizardWorks Group, Inc., 1998.

Feng Shui: Music for Feng Shui and Relaxation. CD. The Mind, Body & Soul Series, New World Music Inc., 1998.

Lillian Too's Feng Shui Space Clearing. Multimedia CD. World of Feng Shui (*www.wofs.com*), 2000.

Web Sites

www.bartlettdesigns.com—Articles and a great bagua diagram at Feng Shui master Stanley Bartlett's site.

www.bloomington.in.us/~9harmony/—Nine Harmonies School of Feng Shui, founded by Carol Bridges. School and registration information.

www.fengshuiguild.com—The Feng Shui Guild's Web site, primarily for practitioners.

www.fengshui-magazine.com—The online home of Britain's *Feng Shui for Modern Living* magazine. Informative articles.

www.fengshui2000.com—The official site of the International Feng Shui Research Design Centre.

www.fsgreetings.com—Free and fun feng shui e-greetings to send and receive. Created with World of Feng Shui (*www.wofs.com*).

✐*www.geofengshui.com*–The site of GEO–Geomancy/ Feng Shui Education Organization's online information center.

✐*www.qi-journal.com*–Home site of *Qi: The Journal of Traditional Eastern Health & Fitness*.

✐*www.raymond-lo.com*–Hong Kong–based Raymond Lo's feng shui site, with information and a list of his services.

✐*www.spaceclearing.com*–Karen Kingston's Space-Clearing site, where you can learn about her philosophies and even become certified as a space-clearing practitioner.

✐*www.spiritweb.org/feng-shui.html*–Informative articles by Jenni Liu.

✐*www.windwater.com*–The Feng Shui Institute of America's online home.

✐*www.wofs.com*–Lillian Too's official Web site, with lots of good information and several places to buy feng shui tools and accessories.

✐*www.wsfs.com*–Founded by Terah Kathryn Collins and Jonathan Hulsh, this is the Western School of Feng Shui.

Appendix C

Decluttering Checklist

Ready to stay on top of clutter on a regular basis? Photocopy this list and use it as your guide. Don't forget to do a space clearing in each area once you've cleared it of clutter!

Clutter Zone	Date of Completion
Driveway	
Garage	
Breezeway	
Front yard	
Porch	
Hallway (including hall table and closet)	
Bookshelves	
Staircases	
Dining room (especially table)	
Kitchen counters	
Kitchen cabinets/junk drawer	
Desk drawers/filing cabinets	
Computer hard drives	
Home office/den	
Living room	
Family room/rec room	

Clutter Zone	Date of Completion
Basement (including under stairs and crawl spaces)	
Laundry room	
Bathroom(s)	
Medicine chest(s)	
Bedroom (especially under bed)	
Bedroom closet(s)	
Attic	
Workbench	
Storage shed	
Garden (weeds)	
Car (including glove compartment and trunk)	
Briefcase	
Purse	
Mental clutter	
Other	

Index

WE HAVE EVERYTHING
FOR HOME IMPROVEMENT!

Everything® Feng Shui Book
    $14.95 ($22.95 CAN) 1-58062-587-8
Everything® Feng Shui Decluttering Book
    $9.95 ($15.95 CAN) 1-59337-028-8
Everything® Fix-It Book
    $14.95 ($22.95 CAN) 1-59337-046-6
Everything® Gardening Book
    $14.95 ($22.95 CAN) 1-58062-860-5
Everything® Homebuilding Book
    $14.95 ($22.95 CAN) 1-59337-037-7
Everything® Home Decorating Book
    $14.95 ($22.95 CAN) 1-58062-885-0
Everything® Landscaping Book
    $14.95 ($22.95 CAN) 1-58062-861-3
Everything® Lawn Care Book
    $14.95 ($22.95 CAN) 1-58062-487-1
Everything® Organize Your Home Book
    $14.95 ($22.95 CAN) 1-58062-617-3

Available wherever books are sold!
To order, call 800-872-5627,
or visit us at everything.com
Everything® and everything.com® are registered trademarks
of F+W Publications, Inc.